I0749785

Administration in Theological Libraries

The Theological Librarian's Handbook —Volume 2

EDITED BY ANDREW KECK

ATLA OPEN PRESS
Chicago - 2021

Published by Atla Open Press, an imprint of the American Theological Library Association (Atla), 200 South Wacker Drive, Suite 3100, Chicago, IL 60606-6701 USA.

Published in the United States of America in 2021.

ISBN-13 978-1-949800-22-7 (PDF)
ISBN-13 978-1-949800-23-4 (EPUB)
ISBN-13 978-1-949800-24-1 (Paperback)

Cover design: Simply Aesthetic Design

Contents

Preface

The *Theological Librarian's Handbook* is a multi-volume introductory and concise guide to theological librarianship intended for library staff who do not possess formal training in the field of library and information science, do not have access to it, or are unable to acquire it in a formal way. Such library staff can often be found in small and emerging theological libraries in the majority world, but also in church and monastery libraries in the West. They are mostly solo librarians with a degree in theology or similar degree in humanities who have been instructed in their job responsibilities by another member of the institution or by an external professional librarian.

This book series is a project of the International Theological Librarianship Education Task Force (ITLE), an international initiative of four theological library associations (Atla, ANZTLA, BETH, and ForAtl) created in 2018. The mission of ITLE is to strengthen and connect theological and religious studies librarians worldwide by identifying resources, creating educational opportunities, and developing skill enhancement materials through collaborative efforts. The idea to produce a book series on the practice of theological librarianship came because of discussions within the task force about the state of theological librarianship worldwide and the understanding that many theological librarians are working in isolation, without access to any form of professional training or support from colleagues.

There are many reasons these librarians do not have professional training today:

- **no access**—the absence of library science programs or library professionals in their working area, or, if a program is available, it is delivered in such a manner that a working librarian is unable to attend classes;

- **too expensive**—in many countries, a professional or master's degree in library science can be very expensive, and the theological librarians or their libraries cannot afford to pay for training;

- **no legal status**—in some countries, religious libraries do not have a clear and recognized status. They are not mentioned in any of the country's laws and standards for libraries, nor do they have a section in their national library associations. Therefore, there is no overarching national institution or law that would require library staff in these libraries to have a professional degree. This is mostly the case with theological libraries belonging to religious communities;

- **no organizations**—the absence of professional theological library associations in a country or region which would organize theological library education workshops and seminars;

- **no motivation**—some institutions to which these libraries belong believe that professional training for work in a theological library is not necessary.

Because of all these reasons, members of ITLE have decided to develop various freely accessible, synchronous and asynchronous means of library education, which will be offered to the international theological library community. This handbook series is one of those means and is primarily addressed to librarians in smaller, more independent libraries, which are not part of university libraries or systems. These would include libraries of seminaries, churches, institutes, etc. Librarians working in such libraries usually have more freedom to implement their own policies and practices but may not be well equipped to formulate them. The handbook seeks to address the most important topics and challenges for their work and give advice on these matters.

This second volume in the series addresses the topic of library administration. Models for the administration of theological libraries vary significantly based on size, location, culture, and context. Commonly, theological libraries must develop an internal administration of policies, procedures, and goals in relation to collection management, staffing/volunteers, planning, reporting, and budget. Library administration is executed within the context of a broader institutional environment that includes reporting relationships, financial accountability, formal library committees, and the broader regulatory environment.

Library administration is a complex area to explore and, while this volume is arranged topically, the authors note a degree of overlap and connection between the various essays. The "budget" is deeply related to "planning and reporting" as well as to "financial accountability." One cannot fully outline the "library policies and procedures" without understanding "library regulations and standards" and the role of the "library committee." "Library mission and goals" represents the start to "planning and reporting" while determining the roles and purpose of "library staff" and "volunteers." Topics in library administration are never completely discrete but are closely related to every other topic within the overall context of library administration.

The authors invite you to explore their essays, as written from various global contexts and perspectives, and use them as a catalyst for developing your own comprehensive vision for library administration. There is no "one way" to administer a theological library, but we trust that you will find some helpful principles, ideas, and examples to consider in these essays. Further, we strongly advocate connecting with library colleagues in similar contexts or a library association. As one joins a broader community of library leaders, the formal and informal dialogues with others will help further illustrate and refine the concepts contained in this volume. We look forward to the ongoing conversations!

MATINA ĆURIĆ (series editor) & ANDREW KECK (volume editor)

CHAPTER 1

Library Mission Statements

AMY LIMPITLAW

NOT LONG AGO, A COLLEAGUE WHO HAS BEEN WORKING FOR THE PAST FEW years as the director of a seminary library related to me her frustrations with the administration at her school. Despite having worked hard to implement new programs, this director was under pressure from the dean to make deep cuts to the library's budget line for collections. With the recent loss of several library staff members due to resignations, there was also pressure on the director to not fill the positions that had been vacated. Her attempts to revise the remaining staff positions to cover the work caused by these vacancies elicited complaints from the staff who remained. In frustration, my colleague told me with dismay that she suddenly realized that all her creative planning for library programs and events mattered not at all to the dean, who, she believed, really just wanted her to spend as little as possible and keep the remaining staff happy and uncomplaining.

In my nearly twenty years as a theological librarian, I have often heard similar grumblings from colleagues about administrators and faculty who just do not quite understand and value the work of the library in the same way that we librarians do. Some of our administrators seem to see us as a repository for physical books and nothing more. I once encountered an administrator who questioned the need for a technical services librarian to catalog the books, not understanding why we just couldn't place them randomly on the shelves after purchasing them! Another time, an administrator at my seminary questioned why we needed to keep buying books at all—didn't we already have plenty? I have also encountered faculty members who distrust the librarians to make appropriate book selections, and, of course, there are all the times we make efforts to provide creative and innovative instructional programs, only to have these efforts overlooked and ignored. Even getting administrators to commit to something as essential as time set aside for library orientation for incoming students can be a challenge when the need for such instruction is not apparent.

But, as my colleague also learned, even library staff members can be so focused on the concerns of their own jobs that they lose sight of the larger purposes for which the library exists. When staff depart and budgets are cut, library staff may need to take on new responsibilities, yet staff can be resistant to these exigencies, especially when they are comfortable within the familiar domains of their own work. Of course, identifying and communicating the larger purposes to which each staff member's work contributes is primarily the responsibility of the director or head librarian. But when higher-ups are not on board with what the director sees as the mission of the library, it is nearly impossible for the director to lead the staff effectively toward that mission.

While a library mission statement is not a panacea for these problems, it can be a helpful step toward clarifying for all parties the library's purpose and priorities. And I would argue that it is not simply the existence of a mission statement that can be helpful, but that the very act of crafting a mission statement can be especially beneficial. Of course, how the mission statement is developed—particularly who contributes and decides on what should be the library's mission—is crucial. In the following, I will make the argument for the benefits not simply of having a clear mission statement, but of doing the hard work of engaging with key stakeholders to develop a mission statement.

Mission statements first became popular in the business world in the early 1980s (Alegra et al. 2018, 456) and were tied to the growing popularity of strategic planning that took off in the 1970s (Vizeu et al., 2013, 179). Academic institutions and libraries subsequently adopted the practice set in motion by the corporate world. Yet, interestingly, the term "mission" is theological in origin, and thus it is perhaps fitting for theological libraries to express an understanding of their purpose in terms of a "mission." As noted by Vizeu and Matitz in an article arguing for the religious origin of organizational and corporate behavior,

> ...the word mission comes from the Latin *mitto*, meaning I send. Originally the term was used to describe the sending of the Son of God, Jesus, to mankind and later the sending of the Holy Spirit to dwell among the Christians. . . . The mission became the essential task of every Christian, according to the directions of the Gospels of the New Testament. (Vizeu et al. 2018, 184)

The idea of "mission" was central to Christianity and informed the idea of evangelization as the work of missionaries who were sent around the world spreading the gospel.

Although the "mission" of the theological library may not be identical to the work of Christian missionaries in spreading the gospel, it is not unrelated. Most theological libraries exist within theological institutions: schools of theology, seminaries, and divinity schools. The work of the library has its own specificity, but it fits within the context of the larger work of its parent institution. And the mission of most theological institutions is related in some sense to the mission of the church—the larger Christian community.

Mission statements communicate an organization's primary purpose and reason for being. Just as the origin of the term "mission" is an active verb—the Latin *missio*—the mission statement describes not simply what the institution is, but what it *does*. The mission statement is not merely descriptive but is proscriptive; it speaks about what the institution's core purpose is and points toward the goals that it must accomplish in order to further this core purpose. The mission statement makes explicit what should be implicit in all the activities of the organization. Although proscriptive in nature, the mission does not need to define in detail how the organization will accomplish its mission, although it may include this information. What is most important is for the mission statement to provide a focus or purpose for the organization.

The theological library's mission should be aligned with the mission of its parent institution. It is not necessarily the same, however, as the seminary or school of theology is different from the library. But the library's mission should cohere with the core mission of its parent institution. The two missions should be compatible with one another and, since the library is subordinate to the parent institution, its mission should serve and support the mission of the school.

In addition to identifying the core purpose of the library, the library's mission statement should also identify the community the library serves. In most cases, for the theological library, this will primarily be the students and faculty of the parent institution, but it may also include other scholars, alumni, and other patrons. Again, because it is important for the library's mission to align with and support the mission of its parent institution, it is helpful for the mission statement to make this connection explicit. And while it is not necessary to define in the mission statement how the library will accomplish its purpose, it can be helpful to include this information.

There is more than one audience for the library's mission statement, and the mission statement may serve different but overlapping purposes for each distinct audience. First, there is the audience of the library staff itself. A mission statement may serve as a statement of identity for the staff, and it may help staff members to recognize how their individual contributions to the work of the library come together for a unified purpose. Mission statements can also help staff prioritize their work, because they can use the mission statement as a benchmark against which they measure the work they are actually doing. In the same way, a mission statement can help staff guard against "mission creep," that is, the tendency to take on more and more tasks that may in fact be extraneous to the central mission of the library (McMullen 2015, 119–210). The mission statement helps to center the staff to understand themselves as part of a single team focused on the same purpose. The mission statement can also help staff be more flexible because it can help them see how modifying how they do their work may be necessary for the sake of adhering to the library's mission, which remains stable and consistent. And if the library's mission statement is aligned with the mission statement of the parent institution, this can help staff to feel more directly a part of the larger educational organization within which the library exists. From experience, I have often observed that library staff can sometimes feel themselves cut off from the rest of the seminary community; a mission statement that connects the library to the seminary can help them feel more directly a part of the larger work of the seminary.

Administrators, especially seminary presidents and deans, are another important audience for the mission statement. The mission statement serves to set forth explicitly what the library's purpose is and, for some administrators, this can be a revelation. During times when schools are under increasing financial pressure, the library can be a tempting target for budget cuts. The value the library provides to the seminary is not always evident to higher-ups in the administration. A mission statement can help to provide a strong defense of the library's necessity and value. Some administrators simply do not fully understand what is involved in the work of the library staff. Some administrators even see the library as no more than a repository for physical books, and thus question the need for the library (and its staff) when there is the Internet. A mission statement, especially if it is explicit about the library's connection to the mission of the school, can serve to mitigate these misunderstandings about the library's importance and value.

A similar case can be made for the purpose the mission statement serves with respect to faculty. As with administrators, faculty may not be aware of how the library contributes to the mission of the school beyond simply obtaining and housing books needed for faculty research and teaching. Although faculty will be less directly involved than administrators in decisions concerning library budgets, when the threat of budget cuts arrives, having faculty on board who support and understand more fully the mission of the library can be of enormous importance.

Similarly, while students would not have the same clout as faculty, it is helpful for students to be aware of the mission of the library. Students will likely have even more direct personal experience of library services and resources than faculty, particularly if they benefit from library instruction and reference services. Similarly, sometimes students are not aware that library staff are there to actually help them. Letting students know that service in support of the students is core to the library's mission through the mission statement will encourage students to take advantage of the services offered by the library, will improve student research and learning, and will in turn increase awareness throughout the school of the library's essential value.

In addition to administrators, faculty, and students, the mission statement can also serve to provide a sense of the library's identity and value to alumni and other potential donors to the school or the library. This last group will probably have the least amount of direct experience with the library's collections and services, which is why having a written statement that clearly explains the library's purpose is even more important in reaching this audience. They may rarely, if ever, enter the library, yet a mission statement can provide them with an understanding of the centrality of the library to the school's mission.

The task of crafting the mission statement is nearly as important as the mission statement itself. As we have seen, there are various stakeholders with an interest in the library: library staff, seminary administrators, faculty, students, alumni. It is crucial, when crafting the library's mission statement, to get input from members of each of these groups. Doing so can be enlightening, especially when what emerges are somewhat different understandings of the library's core activities and purposes. While it can be disturbing to discover that the faculty and administration understand the purpose of the library to be quite different from how the staff see this, having these conversations is important. Such conversations allow for a mutual education. Library staff can educate the faculty and administration about some of the unseen yet vitally important aspects of the library's work, and faculty and administrators can in turn identify their expectations for the library, especially with respect to the library's role in supporting the mission of the school.

In addition to soliciting input from a variety of stakeholders, it can be helpful in crafting the mission statement to consider the mission statements of peer institutions. Most important, of course, is to consider the mission statement of the parent institution and to try to make the connection between the mission of the library and the mission of the seminary explicit in the library's mission statement. While the mission statement itself should be fairly concise, in crafting the mission statement it can be helpful to provide a document that unpacks and explains it in more detail, especially in terms relating it to the mission of the seminary. Finally, after its creation, the mission statement should not be set aside and forgotten but should instead be consulted regularly and used to help determine specific goals. To paraphrase from the words of a dean in describing the mission statement for a seminary, the library mission statement "both reflects and shapes the [library's] commitments, ideally in a continuous process of accountability and revisioning" (Jinkins 2007, 19). In using the mission statement in this way, it may become clear at some point that the library is failing to live up to its mission; but it also may emerge that the library's mission has changed and the mission statement needs to be updated.

Thus, the mission statement serves a number of purposes. It provides a statement that identifies the library by naming its core purpose, and ideally situates that mission in relationship to the mission of its parent institution. The mission statement should both reflect the reality of the library's work and also be proscriptive and even aspirational. The mission statement provides the staff with a shared sense of identity, linking their individual contributions to a united purpose. The mission statement provides a benchmark against which staff can measure their accomplishments and identify priorities. It also serves to set boundaries to the work of the library and to prevent staff from being pulled into activities that are extraneous to the library's mission. Finally, for seminary administrators, faculty, and students, the mission statement helps to make clear the value and centrality of the library to the life of the seminary.

Works Cited

Alegre, Inés, Jasmina Berbegal-Mirabent, Adrián Guerrero, and Marta Mas-Machuca. 2018. "The Real Mission of the Mission Statement: A Systematic Review of the Literature." *Journal of Management and Organization* 24, no. 4: 456–73. *https://doi.org/10.1017/jmo.2017.82*.

Glasrud, Bruce. 2001. "Your Mission Statement has a Mission." *Nonprofit World* 19, no. 5: 35–7.

Jinkins, Michael. 2007. "Mission Possible: Making Use of the School's Mission Statement in Curriculum Review." *Theological Education* 43, no. 1: 17–21.

McMullen, Anthony. 2015. "Mission Creep and Marketing Myopia: Lessons Learned from the Business World." *The Bottom Line* 28, no. 4: 119–21. *https://doi.org/10.1108/BL-07-2015-0011*.

Salisbury, Preston and Matthew R. Girffis. 2014. "Academic Library Mission Statements, Web Sites, and Communicating Purpose." *Journal of Academic Librarianship* 40, no. 6: 59–6. *https://doi.org/10.1016/j.acalib.2014.07.012*.

Vaters, Karl. 2018. "Living Your Library's Passion." *Information Outlook* 22, no. 5: 9–10.

Vizeu, Fabio and Queila Regina Souza Matitz. 2013. "Organizational Sacralization and Discursive use of Corporate Mission Statements." *Brazilian Administration Review* 10, no. 2: 176–94.

Wadas, Linda R. 2017. "Mission Statements in Academic Libraries: A Discourse Analysis." *Library Management* 38, no. 2: 108–16. *https://doi.org/10.1108/LM-07-2016-0054*.

CHAPTER 2

National and International Library Regulations and Standards

ANDREW KECK

PERSONAL LIBRARIES MAY BE ORGANIZED AND MADE AVAILABLE IN ALMOST any way that facilitates storage, discovery, and retrieval by the user. Books might be ordered by size in order to fit into fixed shelving, by subject to enable browsing, or by author/title to allow easy retrieval. Electronic journal articles could be stored in one folder or organized by a citation management system. Organizational schemes can easily be revised, adapted, or abandoned in ways idiosyncratic to the particular user. Library resources need not be arranged at all, allowing for spontaneous discovery and delight.

However, the usefulness of a shared library becomes quickly constrained without some degree of regulation that would be commonly understood among multiple users. With physical books, such regulation could involve a full catalog and classification system, or it could be as simple as arranging books by rough subject, format, or title so that multiple users can find, and potentially add to, the library. With digital items, having some kind of organizational scheme is equally essential—including the metadata to allow for proper discovery and citation.

Regulations and standards become essential when designing cooperative efforts between multiple libraries. The sharing of information and services between libraries requires a common set of definitions and standards. For instance, one cannot create a union catalog between libraries unless there is a standard way of sharing information between libraries and collecting standardized information into the larger effort.

Library regulations and standards run the gamut: technical standards deployed for interlibrary loan software, classification systems that attempt to make sense of the whole of human knowledge, and metadata schema for structuring descriptive records. Library standards also may be created for various library services such as library instruction and collection development. An individual library could engage with almost any number of library regulations and standards propagated by any number of organizations. Some library regulations and standards can be nested so that there may be a broad international standard with more specialized standards that meet specific regional, national, or subject area needs.

International Standards

The broadest international standards are established by the International Organization for Standardization (ISO). Many are irrelevant to libraries (such as sludge recovery), but there are standards regarding languages, bibliographic description, library statistics, publishing statistics, the ISBN, paper quality, and image quality. Most librarians and end users would rarely directly consult these standards—rather they are often built into the products and services regularly used by libraries and librarians. The ISO business model also requires a non-trivial payment for direct access to these standards.

ISO standards and protocols often depend on further standards and protocols in a complex, yet necessary, web of standards.

For example, a protocol such as ISO 18626 for Interlibrary Loan Transactions makes use of at least a dozen additional standards that, in turn, make use of further standards—here are some noted in the ISO 18626 standard (International Organization for Standardization 2017):

- ISO 2108, Information and documentation — International standard book number (ISBN)
- ISO 3166-1, Codes for the representation of names of countries and their subdivisions — Part 1: Country codes
- ISO 3166-2, Codes for the representation of names of countries and their subdivisions — Part 2: Country subdivision code
- ISO 3297, Information and documentation – International standard serial number (ISSN)
- ISO 4217, Codes for the representation of currencies
- ISO 8601, Data elements and interchange formats — Information interchange — Representation of dates and times
- ISO 10957, Information and documentation — International standard music number (ISMN)
- ISO 15511, Information and documentation — International standard identifier for libraries and related organizations (ISIL)
- ISO 8459, Information and documentation — Bibliographic data element directory for use in data exchange and enquiry
- ISO 10160, Information and documentation — Open Systems Interconnection — Interlibrary Loan Application Service Definition
- ISO 10161-1, Information and documentation — Open Systems Interconnection — Interlibrary Loan Application Protocol Specification — Part 1: Protocol specification

- ISO 10161-2, Information and documentation — Open Systems Interconnection — Interlibrary Loan Application Protocol Specification — Part 2: Protocol implementation conformance statement (PICS) proforma

- ISO 20775, Information and documentation — Schema for holdings information

- ISO 23950, Information and documentation — Information retrieval (Z39.50) — Application service definition and protocol specification

Beyond the ISO, a number of other global bodies contribute to the development of international standards of agreements that may be relevant to theological libraries. Intellectual content is regulated by the World Intellectual Property Organization (WIPO) and other organizations establishing standard intellectual property agreements between publishers, authors, and funders. The United Nations Educational, Scientific, and Cultural Organization (UNESCO) develops standards for education and the protection of cultural heritage. The International Council on Archives (ICA) has developed significant archival standards. Particular formats, languages, and cultures may have corresponding bodies or units within larger international bodies that may produce standards with greater granularity.

Among international associations dedicated to libraries, the international body that coordinates library standards is the International Federation of Library Associations and Institutions (IFLA). While behind a number of more technical standards (UNIMARC and FRBR), they also have a number of helpful guidelines for library services, interlibrary loan, authority records, reference service, cataloging, and disaster preparedness (International Federation of Library Associations and Institutions 2021a). Unlike those from the ISO, these regulations and standards are freely available and typically translated in multiple languages. Also within IFLA is a special interest group called Relindial that is specific to religion (International Federation of Library Associations and Institutions 2021b).

Any number of global cooperative projects that are simultaneously standards and tools. A certain degree of standardization is needed to create the tool and, as the tool becomes more widely used, the standards built into the tool become de facto standards. For example, authority records of unique notable name files and numbers are new to international standardization efforts. There is a long history of such authority files being maintained nationally and for obvious reasons of language and national interest. Three related projects have emerged that approach the problem from various vantage points. The International Standard Name Identifier (ISNI) is an ISO effort for uniquely identifying the public identities of contributions to media content. This was developed largely for publishers. A subset of ISNI has been the Open Research and Contributor ID (ORCID) that is focused on scholarly researchers. Finally, the Virtual International Authority File (VIAF) is maintained by OCLC but a joint project of a number of national libraries. Each of these tries to tie standard numbers to individual persons so as to overcome issues with changing names (commonly with marriage), differences in representing the same name/person across cultures/languages, and inconsistencies in presenting the format of names (middle initials, first name abbreviations, etc.).

Regional and National Standards

Regional and national standards typically emerge from a strong national library (or de facto national library), strong national/regional library associations, or national/regional standards organizations. They often attend to peculiarities of language, culture, and geography while promoting cooperation and exchange. Not all nations, national libraries, or organizations promulgate official standards relevant to libraries, and those that do often develop them in concert with international standards.

In the United States, for instance, we have the National Information Standards Organization (NISO) that develops standards related to publishing and libraries. NISO is designated by the American National Standards Institute (ANSI) to contribute to the ISO's work broadly related to publishing and libraries. Countries with larger publishing footprints will typically have at least sub-committees if not separate organizations that develop standards and regulations around publishing.

The Library of Congress, while not officially a national library, often takes a leadership role in creating and promulgating library standards such as a classification system (Library of Congress 2021a), subject headings (Library of Congress 2021b), authority records (Library of Congress 2021c), and more (Library of Congress 2021d). A complex network of various library associations in the United States have developed further standards and regulations. The American Library Association (ALA) has a set of standards (American Library Association 2021) that address many aspects of libraries and have been created by various library divisions, such as the Association of College and Research Libraries. Some standards produced by ALA and its divisions are directly relevant to theological libraries and many are not.

Further, other national organizations may be relevant depending on the type or origin of library materials. The Society of American Archivists looks at archives. Music literature is the topic of the Music Library Association just as art is the topic of the Art Libraries Society of North America. Particularly relevant to theological libraries are the Association of Jewish Libraries, the Catholic Library Association, and Atla. Not all of these organizations produce official standards and regulations. While many are headquartered in, and devote considerable attention to, the United States and the North American context, many seek to engage internationally and have a global impact.

Theological libraries may also be regulated by accreditors and others that regulate educational offerings. The vast majority of active theological libraries are connected to educational institutions and so it is not unusual for "sufficient" library collection and services to be a required part of an accredited educational institution. Within North America, the Association of Theological Schools produces a set of standards of accreditation (Association of Theological Schools 2021) that devotes an entire standard to libraries, with many of the other standards containing items with library implications. Some seminaries may be accredited by a different agency or by more than one accreditor. Seminaries, as educational institutions, may also be subject to state and national regulations. An example of a government regulation that often impacts libraries concerns the privacy of student records and, more broadly, the borrowing history of patrons. While not all countries or regions have accrediting bodies in the same way, there are usually governmental and/or inter-governmental bodies that apply a degree of regulation to educational institutions and, by extension, their libraries.

Finally, theological libraries can be subject to broad sets of regulation and standards related to their facilities (accessibility and fire safety), employees (wage and benefit regulations), finances (reporting of income and expenses), and other aspects of an organization that may be regulated. These regulations can be established at all levels, including local.

Individual Library Adoption of Regulations and Standards

Most standards are not researched and implemented by individual libraries or librarians. Rather, they are researched and implemented by vendors and corporations serving libraries, and there is often a close partnership between library vendors (and their related associations) and the appropriate standards organizations. Library vendors often work on an international basis and make use of international standards promulgated by the ISO and others. Library content contained within databases, books, and journals are also subject to regulations and standards such the International Standard Book Number (ISBN), International Standard Serial Number (ISSN), and the Digital Object Identifier (DOI). Physically published items would be subject to standards for paper, binding, and typography. Digitally published items would be subject to standards for metadata, language encoding, etc.

Similarly, standards related to facilities, employees, finances, and the educational enterprise are more closely attended to by the related educational institution. Individual libraries and librarians have a role in compliance but not primary responsibility. For these kinds of standards, librarians should work carefully with others in the broader organization with responsibilities in these areas. For example, the accounting of financial transactions and signing of contracts should be done in cooperation with the financial office of the institution.

Individual libraries have some choices in the implementation of standards. The classification system, subject headings (or other controlled vocabulary), and, indeed, the primary language of the catalog, is up to each library. Standards on providing reference service are generally voluntary (unless part of accreditation) and so can be implemented wholly, in part, or not at all. Upon investigating standards in any given area, a library may find some are contradictory with one another, inconsistent with other library practices, irrelevant to one's own library, or inappropriate to one's cultural context.

Finally, not every standard is formalized. Atla (formerly the American Theological Library Association) has codified no official standards for theological libraries. Rather, the association promotes research on theological librarianship through Books@ Atla Open Press (the home for this volume), *Theological Librarianship*, annual conference presentations, professional development opportunities, and discussion groups. A very common way of developing standards and best practices in libraries is through research, presentation, conversation, and exchange with other librarians. While not always codified into an official standard, the "idea" of one library is often spread to other libraries through these professional and informal networks.

Conclusion

In conclusion, library regulations and standards promote cooperation and best practices. Theological libraries automatically and unknowingly use a great number of standards through library vendors and cooperative projects. Libraries are also partners in meeting the required regulations and standards of their broader or related organizations. In some areas, libraries and librarians may have autonomy to implement or choose among standards developed at international, regional, national, and local levels. Finally, many "best practices" emerge not as formal standards but from sustained exchange with colleagues.

Works Cited

American Library Association. 2021. "ALA Standards & Guidelines." *Tools, Publications & Resources. https://www.ala.org/tools/guidelines/standardsguidelines.*

Association of Theological Schools. 2021. "Standards | The Association of Theological Schools." *https://www.ats.edu/accrediting/standards.*

International Federation of Library Associations and Institutions. 2021a. "IFLA — Current IFLA Standards." *https://www.ifla.org/node/8750.*

———. 2021b. "IFLA — Religions: Libraries and Dialogue Special Interest Group." *https://www.ifla.org/relindial.*

International Organization for Standardization. 2017. "ISO 18626:2017(En), Information and Documentation — Interlibrary Loan Transactions." *https://www.iso.org/obp/ui/#iso:std:iso:18626:ed-2:v1:en.*

Library of Congress. 2021a. "Classification - Cataloging and Acquisitions (Library of Congress)." *https://www.loc.gov/aba/cataloging/classification.*

———. 2021b. "Controlled Vocabularies | Librarians and Archivists | Library of Congress." *https://www.loc.gov/librarians/controlled-vocabularies.*

———. 2021c. "Catalogs, Authority Records — Cataloging and Acquisitions (Library of Congress)." *https://www.loc.gov/aba/cataloging/authority.*

———. 2021d. "Standards | Librarians and Archivists | Library of Congress." *https://www.loc.gov/librarians/standards.*

CHAPTER 3

Library Policies and Procedures

KATHARINA PENNER

THEOLOGICAL LIBRARIANS FACE MANY DECISIONS DURING THEIR COMPLEX work and often intellectually stretching activities. Policies and procedures come in to provide some order, logic, and predictability. Young institutions will place much less emphasis on policy writing and rather first experiment with various ideas and approaches before documenting successful processes into the form of a policy.[1] The need for policies arises more urgently when the number of staff and offered services grows—a one-person library that provides a few basic services will be less under pressure to spell out details in a written policy. While library policies and procedures in a theological school are important for quality services, to write, discuss and communicate them are often neglected tasks. They fall under the table when library staff is pressed to "get the job done."

While policies explain the "why" of a service or activity, the procedures spell out the "how" in more detail. A policy will set out a framework, goals and objectives to guide decisions on a library service, and be supported, then, by one or several procedures that standardize repetitive tasks through further (practical) details. The collection development policy will, for example, be spelled out in more detail through several procedures, such as a procedure on selection (who selects/approves titles to be added to the collection and how), on acquisition (who acquires approved titles, when, and how), on weeding/deselection, on cataloging, on receiving and processing purchase suggestions (from faculty, students, other users), and many other details. While procedures need to be reviewed and adapted quite frequently, depending on changes in and around the library, policies are more stable defining documents.

Need for Policies in a Theological Library

Much can be said from a theological perspective to justify the need and explain the benefits of well-written policies. Stewardship is an important aspect in a usually under-resourced new library, especially in the majority world, and so policies help to prioritize time and financial expenditures. This is done with sober and mutual judgement; policies should be deliberated over and formulated in a team to prevent decisions made subjectively on the spur of the moment and with insufficient discernment. Policies call staff to integrity. They also demonstrate integrity to users through predictability, consistency, and transparency of processes as expectations and operating methods are disclosed and spelled out. The library creates policies in order to engage in clear and open communication while striving to comply with existing laws.

Policies present the legal framework of a library, including its values, priorities, reasons for decisions, and processes for conflict resolution. Library staff are empowered through policies to implement the mutually decided philosophy of service, to deal with confusing situations or even crises, and to speak with authority with "difficult" or advantage-taking users. While each library has many informal and unwritten policies, having them collected in writing can better ensure continuity and ease the entry for new staff and leadership who receive guidelines as they learn the ropes.[2]

Accreditation agencies place a high importance on policies, including library policies. They will look for correlations between the parent organization's and the library's mission and vision statement, analyze how the library's goals and objectives are reflected in the policies and procedures, and seek evidence of how library policies and their everyday implementation contribute to student learning and the achievement of program outcomes defined by the institution. In accreditation, the burden of proof is on the institution and library and so it needs to find sufficient evidence to demonstrate how it accomplishes its mission and objectives through having well-written policies that correlate with useful measurable implementation.

Purpose and Rationale of Policies and Procedures

The American Library Association summarizes the purpose of library policies as follows (ALA, 2019):

- define the values of the organization
- help managers and staff translate those values into services
- establish a standard for services that can be understood by users of the service and providers
- ensure equitable treatment for all
- provide a framework for delivery of services
- organize library operations in compliance with relevant local, regional, and state laws

Policies can be compared to scaffolding—a structure and a framework with the security and protection in which quality services can be offered. Policies, however, also mean limitations; as soon as something is explicitly stated, something else is excluded. If too many aspects of a library's operation are defined (possibly in strict terms), users' access might be limited and staff might feel limited in how to respond equitably to ad hoc non-standard requests or unanticipated situations. If too few aspects are reflected in the policies or wording is vague and unclear, decisions need to be made spontaneously, possibly under pressure, and possibly reinventing the wheel for the umpteenth time. This might work well in a small library where it is easier to be flexible, negotiate needs and services, and quickly react to an arising situation in an unordinary way without limiting service for other users. Policies need to be as broad as possible (envisioning various scenarios and allowing effective functioning in unpredictable contexts) and as specific as necessary.

Beside shortage of time and perceived (or real) inexperience, which are probably the strongest deterrents in policy writing, other objections are also brought forward. Some believe that the more rules exist, the more stressful the life of a librarian becomes because rules, once created, need to be consistently enforced, independently of time pressures and other (necessary and constructive) library work. Policies are accused of stifling natural processes and inhibiting innovations while enforcing the status quo. Theological schools that find themselves in non-welcoming or outright hostile environments hesitate to openly spell out details of their operations. Sometimes administrators will also be hesitant to say things too clearly in order not to lose support or students.[3]

While devising policies, a library will need to find a delicate balance, useful for its context and culture and suitable for the nature of its parent institution. A balance between too many and too few policies, between policies and user needs, between people-orientation and goal-orientation, between openness to an arising situation and predictabile administrative governance. Policies should never be considered as weapons—neither instruments of power to be wielded over the user, nor instruments of defense against accusations and user complaints. Both aspects do arise, and policies can help solve these conflicts, but this is not the primary purpose for which they are created.

Writing and Revising Policies

Policy writing and revision is guided by considerations, such as

- meeting the users' academic and ministerial needs (usually students, faculty and staff)
- contributing to student learning
- correlating library operations with the mission, vision and values of the institution
- helping to achieve library objectives

When writing policies, it is helpful to start with the end in mind: Will this policy contribute to the mission of the library and institution, to student learning, and to the library functioning as an educational partner? The policy will need to be embedded into the overall culture of the library and institution, as well as considering relevant aspects arising from assessment. Assessment provides an evidence-based evaluation (a glimpse) of the current situation—what services run well, what needs to change. One would first consider whether a problem can be solved through adapting existing policies before creating an additional document. Sometimes, it is useful to prominently highlight an important issue by having a separate policy on it (for example, cellphones in the library).

Policies will be helpful only if they are known and owned by all relevant stakeholders. The person or body to whom the library is responsible will want to know and approve the contents of the policies. There may be a formal process for discussing and adopting (signing into law) a library policy. A library will also consider effective ways to inform and remind its users of the policy contents: a policy manual on display for users, pertinent signs, and/or a policies document on the library website and/or intranet.

Policies will be helpful only if they are relevant and current, meaning that they need to be regularly reviewed and adapted. Revisions might be required because of changes in the library itself, in the parent institution, in the surrounding environment or country laws. The COVID-19 pandemic has caused much soul-searching in 2020 concerning policies and much creative rethinking, without really having useful data at hand, in order to safely adapt library operations. Recommendations changed very quickly, and libraries translated them into policies, some short-lived and some that will remain longer because they have been proven as agents for innovation.

List of Important Policies

Basically, every service or library activity will need to be reflected in one of the existing policies or to receive its own. Some services and processes will possibly need an accompanying detailed procedure. A library might not want to have a flurry of documents—they are time-consuming to produce, follow and reinforce—but it is also not wise to include too many not-directly related aspects into one lengthy policy document.

Some policies will certainly be unique to the specific context of a library but, because many operations are similar in all libraries, it is useful to analyze policy samples from different theological schools on various continents. Many aspects have already been well-formulated elsewhere and can be adjusted and integrated into one's own policy, though certainly not without considering the different contexts, educational cultures, and environments in which a school and library operate.[4]

Important areas that require policies are listed below in no special sequence as they serve as examples and are not exhaustive; each library will need to discuss and decide which documents are required by law and are beneficial to guarantee well-functioning operations.

Collection Development

A collection development policy is probably not the first policy document that a library designs,[5] but it is a very foundational one. It delineates the rationale behind selection and acquisition decisions for a library's print and electronic resources of all document types and who is involved in what role(s) in these decisions.[6] The document will also include a gift and donation policy, a policy on weeding/deselection, and a policy that sets out how objections/challenges to included materials will be handled.[7] If the library is responsible for the institutional archives or special collections, this will be reflected here or in a separate document.[8]

Access to and Use of the Library

Policies in this area will need to be in place before a library starts allowing users access to and use of, including borrowing from, the library. A circulation policy can be part of it or a separate document. An access and use policy defines various user categories with their respective borrowing privileges. In a theological school, these would be faculty, students (resident, full-time, distance, online, from satellite locations), staff, possibly community/external users, students and faculty of neighboring institutions, and "guests" (one-time walk-in users). There might already exist unwritten practices and access terms for these categories, but it is important to spell out in detail what services each user category can expect and at what cost.

Each library has the right to limit library use to certain persons or categories but needs to specify when and why (on what basis) restrictions come into effect (for example, unpaid overdue fees, disregard of existing policies, non-compliance with copyright and download restrictions, etc.). There might be restrictions for external users: in religious institutions, for example, it might be important to justify why a (new or small) library can serve only a limited faith-based or denominationally-related clientele.[9]

If a library is charged with serving distance and online students, access and services for them are spelled out in detail either in this policy or in a separate document.[10]

The use of printers/copiers located in a library, reservation of study space/cabins in the library can be part of the policy or receive special mention in a separate document.

This policy will also need to reflect various aspects of responsible conduct in a library (food and drink, personal belongings, noise, use of cellphones, child safety/unattended children in the library, etc.). Especially in 2020, many hygiene prescriptions were added for staff and users (hand sanitizing, social distancing, use of community computers and study desks, book quarantines after return, high-touch surfaces etc.).

Circulation/Borrowing

A detailed circulation policy spells out the borrowing terms for internal and external users. As mentioned above, different categories of users might receive different privileges and fines, so overdue fines and how they are enforced will be addressed here. Libraries tend to allow longer loan periods for faculty, sometimes also differentiate between several categories of students. External/community users might have specific terms. Sometimes there are variations in loan length during the semester, summer/winter breaks, exam periods, or other special times. Variations also occur for the length of time different types of materials (DVDs, journals, etc.) circulate. As mentioned above, the more variations, the more there is to remember and enforce, so these need to be justified and contribute to the equity of use for all patrons.

Beside study resources, a library might decide to make available various devices, such as laptops, iPads, Kindles with e-books, USB drives, and other items. The loan terms for these might be part of the general circulation policy but receive a separate procedural document.

Resource Sharing

No library is self-sufficient, and so agreements with accompanying policies and procedures will be required for interlibrary loan, document delivery, and collaborative collection development in a consortium.[11] Some of these aspects might be part of collection development (Collaborative CD), the circulation policy (for example, ILL), or be stand-alone documents. The resource-sharing processes, negotiated between the libraries, will require clearly stated guidelines and demarcations of responsibilities, consideration of legal restrictions, and the allocation of necessary finances in the budget. Each process may require a detailed procedure.

Information Competence Training

Policies in this domain of library work might have different names, such as information literacy policy, library instruction, and user training. They are often devised together with the teaching faculty and read more like an educational framework (with mission, goals and objectives, content, various levels of intervention, and dates of instruction). Each activity/intervention might need a separate policy and procedure, for example, new students' library orientation, various library workshops, course-embedded library instruction, personal instruction/tour of library, and others.[12]

Technological Infrastructure

This is an umbrella term for technological processes for which the library is responsible, such as automation (Integrated Library System), library computers, electronic resources, information security (management of passwords), library website, social media activities, digitization activities, and/or a possible institutional repository operated by the library. The titles of the policies and procedures will vary accordingly. Policies in this area will be devised in cooperation with information technology (IT) and/or other departments. They will reflect the library's section while being correlated with the overall IT policy of the parent institution.

Integrity Issues

The question of academic integrity and copyright infringement will need to be addressed in one of the policies. Possibly there already is an institutional "Academic Integrity Policy" in place that also specifies the library's contribution in addressing the problem.[13] It doesn't hurt, however, to additionally emphasize these aspects in other documents.

Another important aspect in this category is the confidentiality and security of patron records. Regulated in various ways in each country, the library will need to comply with the laws and inform patrons of its efforts in this.

Clarifying decent treatment of human resources, a library might consider writing a policy on how it handles student staff and/or volunteers or how professional development for its staff is organized.

Safety and Security Issues

Safety and security issues in a library mainly concern the protection of people (users and staff), of holdings and facilities/equipment, and Internet-related aspects. These might already be covered in other important library or institutional documents, such as a library access and use policy, campus safety policy, or IT policy. A library would then need to develop a procedure on the basis of these documents for steps of action or routines to follow in case of incidents and emergencies on its premises. The procedure would include safety resources, such as contact details of responsible personnel, police and ambulance phone numbers, evacuation routes, and other important details.

Possibly the institution will already have a disaster and emergency plan that pays attention to library specifics, though this is not a given. Even though no one wishes for such tragedies to happen, it is not uncommon that natural and human-made catastrophes damage library holdings and jeopardize people's lives, and so it is vital to have a disaster response and recovery plan in place before the calamity strikes.

Conclusion

Usually policy documents, together with the more detailed procedures, will be combined into a library's policy manual (or a library operations manual) for everyday referral by all stakeholders. Possibly two policy manuals are necessary, one for users and a more extensive one for library staff.

For a new library, the best advice is to start such a manual as soon as possible with the most foundational and urgent policies and keep adding to it. For an already existing library, it is a very worthwhile, though time-consuming, task to bring all written and unwritten policies and procedures together in one place to collaboratively examine what already exists, where the gaps are, where contradictions are observed in different policies, and whether procedures and actual operations correlate with the policies. Policies can positively affect institutional culture if they reflect and integrate the values, traditions and practices of the library.

Works Cited

ALA. 2019. "Library Policy Development." *https://libguides.ala.org/librarypolicy.*

Illinois University Library. 2020. "A Quick Reference Guide to Developing Library Policies and Procedures." *https://guides.library.illinois.edu/writing-library-policies.*

IFLA. 2001. "Guidelines for a Collection Development Policy using the Conspectus Model." *https://www.ifla.org/publications/guidelines-for-a-collection-development-policy-using-the-conspectus-model.*

Jaeger, John. 2003. "Plagiarism on the Internet." *Christian Librarian* 46, no. 2. *https://digitalcommons.georgefox.edu/tcl/vol46/iss2/4.*

Mayer, Robert J. 2018. "Theological Librarians and Collection Management: Collaborative Policy Development." *Theological Librarianship* 11, no. 2: 8–11. *https://doi.org/10.31046/tl.v11i2.530.*

Smiley, Bobby, ed. 2019. *Information Literacy and Theological Librarianship: Theory & Praxis.* Chicago: Atla Open Press. *https://doi.org/10.31046/atlaopenpress.33.*

Sweeney, Julie E. 2020 "And Our Neighbors as Ourselves? Serving Unaffiliated Patrons in Christian Library Consortium Libraries." *Christian Librarian* 63, no. 2. *https://digitalcommons.georgefox.edu/tcl/vol63/iss2/6.*

Notes

1 Many majority-world theological schools, especially in oral cultures, have only very few written library policies, usually for foundational everyday services. Other policies are transmitted orally and can be quickly adapted. There might also be some fear of becoming "locked in" through writing.

2 Written collections/manuals of policies are very important in times of staff changes and during introductions of new staff. They offer a one-stop place to become acquainted with the status quo in order to ensure a smooth transition and predictable continuation of services. They also provide the foundation for refining and reviewing existing policies and procedures against changing contexts.

3 For example (real case), a multi-denominational theological school in Ukraine that has to carefully watch its standing with different denominations will avoid including all-too-clear statements in its collection development policy about the denominational alignment of its resources. By necessity, wording will be vague so that if materials are challenged there is nothing on paper that would cause bad publicity and jeopardize support. A Christian theological school in Central Asia will write down as little as possible about its collection and not display it in an online catalog so as not to raise flags for government officials.

4 Helpful advice, samples, and legal guidance can often be found on websites of library associations, national and international, from university and theological libraries. The national library of a country and the ministry of education (or culture) will be useful resources. There are also sample policies in books on librarianship or library guides on the Internet, for example, *https://libguides.ala.org/librarypolicy* or *guides.library.illinois.edu/writing-library-policies.*

5 In a recent discussion with several librarians from majority-world theological libraries, we realized that none of us had a written collection development policy. But all of these libraries had well balanced collections and provided more or less sufficient resources to support the curriculum. When trying to establish the reasons for their success with a functioning collection, created without a policy, several markers stood out as significant: well-established communication

with each department, committed involvement of faculty in the selection of sources, and long-term continuity in acquisitions because the lead librarians were part of the institution for over fifteen years.

6 See some guidance from IFLA in several languages: *https://www.ifla.org/publications/guidelines-for-a-collection-development-policy-using-the-conspectus-model.*

7 This topic will be discussed in much more detail in the third volume of the *Theological Librarian's Handbook*, forthcoming in 2022.

8 See a helpful description of the revision process of a CD policy in Robert J. Mayer (2018).

9 See a helpful discussion starter with a literature review and various current policies and practices on faith-based institutions serving unaffiliated patrons in Sweeney (2020).

10 Many worthwhile materials have been published in the last 10–15 years on this topic. See also several entries in *Theological Librarianship*, vol. 13, no. 2 (2020), where authors reflect on their special services for distance students in general and how they coped with the COVID-19 pandemic, where all students were suddenly online students.

11 Consortial agreements might necessitate the creation of additional policies. While the agreement regulates the relationship(s), the area, and the process of mutual cooperation, the implementation and use of consortial benefits might need to be spelled out for local staff in an additional policy. Alternatively, already existing policies can be expanded to include relevant references to consequences from a consortial agreement.

12 See the very useful volume from Atla Open Press on *Information Literacy and Theological Librarianship*, edited by Bobby Smiley (2019).

13 As John Jaeger underlines, the purpose of such policies is not to threaten students or prevent plagiarism by fear of being caught and punished. They should rather serve an educational purpose and emphasize formation toward a Christian worldview and values, such as wholeness, honesty and integrity, responsibility and creativity, and desire for the development of qualitative new knowledge (Jaeger 2003).

CHAPTER 4

Mentoring and Supervising Library Staff in a Theological Library

JAEYEON LUCY CHUNG

NEW AND EMERGING LIBRARY LEADERS, AS WELL AS THOSE WHO START A new theological library, often wonder what it takes to manage library personnel effectively and equitably. Whether a library director manages multiple employees or just one, supervising and mentoring library staff with different personality types, learning goals, and professional needs are not easy tasks. Particularly in a theological library setting where financial and human resources are limited and yet high performance and productivity are demanded, motivating library workers to achieve the organization's goals and fulfill their own potential can be quite challenging. How is it possible to develop and implement a model of library management that empowers both organizational growth and individual growth? This question has been central to the author, who has directed the Styberg Library of Garrett-Evangelical Theological Seminary since 2012. Based on her nine-year library management experience, the author in this chapter aims to present a relational and inclusive model of staff supervision and mentoring. While one model that has grown in a specific context cannot be universally applied to all settings, the author hopes that the model and practices represented here provide emerging and new library leaders with some insights and guidelines.

To give a brief description of the author's institution—Garrett-Evangelical Theological Seminary, with a long history of 168 years, is a freestanding United Methodist seminary located on the campus of Northwestern University in the north suburbs of Chicago. The Styberg Library serves mainly the students, faculty, staff, and alumni of Garrett but, as an affiliate of Northwestern's library system, it also provides services to the Northwestern community as well as local clergy and researchers. Committed to serving everyone professionally, hospitably, and equitably in a welcoming environment, the Styberg Library aspires to advance the educational mission of Garrett by expanding access, enhancing the teaching and learning process, empowering research, and facilitating collaboration. The library is largely organized into four areas: collection development and acquisitions, cataloging and metadata, access and public services, and library instruction and technology. There are currently four full-time professional librarians, including the director, and one full-time paraprofessional staff. Prior to the COVID-19 pandemic, the library had an additional workforce—fourteen or fifteen graduate students working ten hours weekly in a variety of roles—which would be most likely reinstated in a post-pandemic era. The library director reports to the vice president for academic affairs.

A relational-inclusive model of staff supervision and mentoring is currently limited to full-time library staff while it can be applied to student workers. Focusing on an organic relationship between organizational growth and individual growth, this model identifies five key guiding principles such as: 1) clear and open communication, 2) professional development and growth, 3) fairness and reciprocity, 4) hospitable and inclusive space, and 5) teamwork and shared responsibility. These values have emerged inductively from concrete processes and experiences, and each will be briefly discussed in the next section. In order for the readers to understand how each principle can be materialized in actual practices, the author will illustrate some examples which have been implemented in the Styberg Library.

A Relational-Inclusive Model of Staff Supervision and Mentoring — Five Guiding Principles and Practices

Influenced by transformational leadership theory, which James MacGregor Burns initially introduced in 1978 (Burns 1978) and Bernard Bass later expanded (Bass and Riggio 2006), the author calls her model of staff supervision and mentoring a relational-inclusive model. Similar to the theory of transformational leadership, this model focuses on providing a clear vision and goals for the library, offering individualized support and mentoring to each staff, and fostering creativity and innovative thinking. In order to empower individuals and facilitate positive changes in the library, the relational-inclusive model especially emphasizes the significance of creating and nurturing an open and inclusive space among library staff. This model is composed of five primary guiding principles, which are organically interconnected to one another and helpful in carrying out the model practically.

First, *clear and open communication*. The author begins with two questions here. What is communication and why is it important? According to the *Merriam-Webster Dictionary*, communication has two meanings: 1) a process by which information is exchanged between individuals through a common system of symbols, signs, or behavior; 2) personal rapport (Merriam-Webster Dictionary n.d.). Communication is important, since it can promote or impede the cognitive understanding or relational quality between people. Oftentimes, people in the leadership position think of communication as giving a command or delivering a message unilaterally. Closed, unilateral, and unclear communication causes confusion, powerlessness, and compartmentalization among individuals and within the group. On the contrary, open, bilateral, and clear communication encourages understanding, agency, and connection. Genuine and mutual communication enables listening with care and speaking with clarity so that individual staff members can experience a relational-inclusive culture within their team.

Regular weekly and monthly meetings are practices that the author's library has established to advance open and qualitative communication among staff. At first, Monday weekly meetings, thirty minutes long, started as a way to communicate to one another what would happen in the library in general and in each person's area in particular. Monthly meetings, sixty to ninety minutes long, were also scheduled to discuss a variety of library-related agendas in more detail and depth. The initial purpose of these meetings was to ensure that the tasks and projects meet deadlines and to share information for collaboration and support. Gradually, these meetings have also become a space to connect and engage with one another by sharing personal stories of joy and sadness. The entire team would celebrate any individual person's achievements or happy news together. When a staff person lost their family member, other staff members would step up to comfort the grieving person and offer assistance to cover their chat shift or other duties. Clear and open communication cultivates a community of trust and collegiality.

Second, *professional development and growth*. As indicated in the introduction, a relational-inclusive model emphasizes an organic relationship between institutional growth and individual growth. Traditionally, librarians have been considered as gatekeepers of informational resources or maintainers of the status quo. In a relational-inclusive model, however, librarians perceive themselves as lifelong learners, community builders, and change makers. Their ongoing development and maturation, in this view, is key to advancing the mission of the library as well as fulfilling their own potential and goals. To be more specific, professional development and growth may be equated with attending a professional conference, presenting a paper, or taking a profession-related course. From the author's perspective, professional development and growth is quintessentially a relational concept, which is enabled by mutual attention and interest between two individuals—a supervisor-mentor and a staff-mentee. Professional growth does not happen in an isolated, privatized setting; rather, it takes place in the mutual space where a mentee shares goals and aspirations, and a mentor listens and responds with care.

To approach staff management and development from the perspective of a relational-inclusive model, the author's library launched a cyclical mentoring system that involves a goal conference, individual consultations, and performance reviews. At the beginning of each fiscal year (early July), a library director and an individual staff member meet to discuss individual goals that have already been identified by the staff. They also discuss the staff's timelines and action plans as well as the library priorities. The staff finalizes the goals based on the conversation with the supervisor. Throughout the year, the staff schedules individual consultations with the supervisor once or twice per month to discuss the progress or challenges, and the supervisor offers a listening ear and constructive feedback or needed support. A performance review, which is usually scheduled in late spring or early summer, depending on the seminary's schedule, focuses mainly on the staff person's growth and development while also celebrating the successful completion of tasks and projects. When a goal is not accomplished due to an unexpected situation, it will be carried over to the next year's list of goals.

Third, *fairness and reciprocity*. Concepts of fairness and reciprocity are interrelated and critical in actualizing a relational-inclusive model. While the notion of fairness can be interpreted in several different ways, the author, in the context of library management, defines it as equal treatment of individuals. Fairness refers to just and impartial treatment of people without prejudice or discrimination based on their identity, background, rank, or other social factors. The principle of fairness does not exclude the fact that there are differences in positions, roles, and responsibilities within the library. Yet, it affirms that each member of the group is treated justly, their voices are given equal respect, and opportunities for development are offered fairly. In this situation, fairness proliferates reciprocity within the group. The idea of reciprocity refers to the practice of interchanging mutual respect and equal treatment for one another. Fairness and equitable treatment are expected reciprocally between individuals or groups.

Then, how can the principle of fairness and reciprocity be embodied in a concrete situation? While fairness and reciprocity can be experienced in supervisory relationships or group interactions, they can also be demonstrated in the written documents such as a library staff handbook. The handbook is often considered as a way of setting and enforcing rules and policies, but it can also be utilized as a means of conveying such relational and communal values as fairness and reciprocity. The Styberg Library's handbook indicates that all library staff members are fairly provided one development hour per week during their work hours. How they use their development hour is an individual's choice. They sometimes decide to attend a webinar, audit a seminary course, or read a journal article. The handbook also states that each staff person is provided an equal amount of professional development funding. While the amount varies year by year, it communicates that each member's professional needs matter and receive equal attention.

Fourth, *hospitable and inclusive space.* How one creates and nourishes a hospitable and inclusive space within the library team is fundamental to actualizing a relational-inclusive model. Many contemporary libraries are aware of the diversity among the populations they serve and try to develop a service model that recognizes the differences and represents inclusivity for their communities. Library workers are expected to serve as joyful agents of welcome and friendliness while providing a safe and hospitable space to all users. Interestingly enough, it is not much emphasized that library staff also need to experience the power of a hospitable and inclusive space themselves and be nurtured in that space. A hospitable and inclusive space enables individuals to explore and express their ideas and feelings freely and openly, without worry or anxiety. It also helps them foster mutual recognition and acceptance despite their differences. Building such a space does not happen automatically or overnight; it takes some intentional efforts.

While hospitality and inclusivity can be practiced in all sorts of daily relational encounters and group interactions, strategically devised activities can contribute to further solidifying the germinating culture of hospitality. Among multiple activities that the author's library has conducted are annual retreats, staff birthday parties, and end-of-semester staff appreciation breakfasts. Particularly, annual library retreats take place for a day typically in mid-summer. Each year, the theme for a retreat varies, yet such items—visioning and strategic planning process, discovering self and others, picnic or field trip—are usually included. At the most recent retreat, library staff had an opportunity to take Myers Briggs Type Indicator (MBTI) personality tests and share their findings, which helped to understand one another better. The library team also took a field trip to a local museum and archives, which opened an opportunity not only to learn the local history but also to simply enjoy themselves in accompaniment with others.

Last, *teamwork and shared responsibility*. Building a mutual relationship and an inclusive space within the library leads to teamwork and shared responsibility. If the preceding four principles focus more on the process, the final principle of teamwork and shared responsibility demonstrates the outcome. As one can imagine, teamwork and shared responsibility cannot be expected in a circumstance where open and clear communication is not practiced, individual growth and development is not encouraged; fair treatment and reciprocity is not experienced, and a hospitable and inclusive space is not built. Only when those four principles are in operation, library team members can finally start participating in teamwork and sharing responsibilities for the common good, even if it means having to learn new skills, covering someone else's shifts, or reorganizing normal work schedules. The principle of teamwork and shared responsibility becomes truly critical, especially in crisis or unprecedented situations.

For instance, during the pandemic which started in March 2020, the Styberg Library had to confront and respond to unseen challenges and barriers, just like most other libraries around the globe. Three months after the complete shutdown of the campus, library staff were allowed to go back to the library so that they could provide its user community with limited physical services such as curbside pickup, scanning, and ILL. While the library had developed clear guidelines and procedures for safety and workflows before resuming those limited services, it was still an uncomfortable and fearful situation. It also meant that they all had to perform circulation duties when working in the library every other week, regardless of their normal responsibilities. What the library team has embodied and represented for the past few months is the spirit of teamwork and shared responsibility. For the collective good of the library and its community, they readjusted their work schedules and reorganized their priorities and workflows willingly. With an outstanding and faithful service to users, the library is now perceived as the symbolic center of the seminary by many.

Conclusion

Above, the author illustrated a relational-inclusive model as an effective and equitable model of staff supervision and mentoring. With a purpose to accomplish organizational goals and, at the same time, fulfill individual potential, the author emphasized a relational-inclusive model as critical to fostering agency and creativity as well as to facilitating positive changes within the library. The author also presented five key guiding principles—open and clear communication, professional development and growth, fairness and reciprocity, hospitable and inclusive space, and teamwork and shared responsibility—as tools to carry out a relational-inclusive model in concrete situations. A few practices that have been developed and implemented in the author's library context were suggested as examples.

As the author mentioned previously, this relational-inclusive model and its five guiding principles have been identified and redefined in a specific library context through observations and reflections. They also went through modifications as a response to constant changes from the internal and external environments. Some principles and practices may be relevant to some libraries while others may not. It is the author's hope that the readers can critically appropriate some of the ideas presented here in their specific situations.

Works Cited

Burns, James MacGregor. 1978. *Leadership.* New York: Harper Torchbooks.

Bass, Bernard, and Ronald Riggio. 2006. *Transformational Leadership.* Mahwah, NJ: Lawrence Erlbaum Associates, Inc.

Merriam-Webster Dictionary, s.v. "communication," accessed January 20, 2021, *https://www.merriam-webster.com/dictionary/communication.*

CHAPTER 5

Volunteers in Libraries: Friends or Foes?

KELLY CAMPBELL

VOLUNTEERS CAN BE A VALUABLE RESOURCE FOR LIBRARIES. THEY CAN HELP in various areas, including serving on a governing board, providing programming, working at the circulation desk, shelving materials, and even fundraising. In seminary and religious libraries, money and staff are stretched thin. The temptation to start utilizing volunteers without thoughtfully thinking through the benefits and challenges of volunteers can result in library staff and volunteers' needs and expectations being unfulfilled. Therefore, this chapter will explore issues to be thoughtfully considered before starting a volunteer program. A successful volunteer program is beneficial to the library and rewarding for the volunteer, but it takes knowledge and planning.

Definition of a Volunteer

In the past, the definition of a volunteer was quite simple. He or she was identified as an individual who helped or volunteered with an organization like a library without any expectation of payment for his or her services. The volunteer was expected to do whatever was needed whenever it was needed. Today, however, the definition is changing as people are becoming busier and living more demanding lives. The new breed of volunteers has many obligations and are often involved with multiple organizations. Current volunteers approach volunteerism with a different mindset and possess a specific set of expectations for their volunteer experience. Successful volunteer programs need to adapt to the changes and recognize the seismic shift in volunteerism and the call for an expanded definition of a volunteer.

A characteristic of the new breed of volunteers is that they demand flexibility in tasks and schedules. Rather than being recruited to "volunteer" as a need arises, libraries now ask volunteers how they want to be involved in helping the library. Volunteers are empowered to work in their own way and according to their own schedules. In the past, volunteers were recruited for the long term and expected to fit within the library's stated needs. This practice is being replaced as volunteers are no longer recruited for a preset slot or function. The mindset that a volunteer has to fit within the library program or structure is gone. This new breed of volunteers expects the library to mold the program or structure to the volunteer's strengths and time commitment as he or she helps the library fulfill its mission.

In addition to the characteristic of flexibility, this new breed of volunteer is interested in episodic volunteering, a trend that has increased since 1989. Episodic volunteers prefer short-term volunteer projects rather than long-term commitments. Long-term commitment volunteers are from a different generation than the present one. A study titled *Volunteer Growth in America: A Review of Trends in Volunteering Since 1974*, conducted by the Corporation for Community and National Service (2006), confirms this volunteering trend. Despite the changes expected by this new breed of volunteers, this study found that volunteering rates appear to be at a thirty-year high. The last fifteen years reflect the changes in how people are donating time and energy to libraries.

Seventy-nine percent of non-volunteers said they would volunteer if given a short-duration task (8). While this study focused on volunteer growth in America, all librarians hoping to start a successful volunteer program need to consider these growing trends and contextualize their volunteer experiences.

Many of this new breed of volunteers are successful professionals with a variety of skills. These professionals serving as volunteers want the respect afforded to professionals. They want their skills to be acknowledged—they do not want to be micromanaged. These types of volunteers are called knowledge workers. Knowledge workers want to make decisions, to be empowered, and to influence how the project assigned to them is accomplished. These professionals want to give back by volunteering; however, since they are successful in their respective fields, they are intolerant of paid staff who are disorganized, who assign them demeaning tasks, and who fail to follow through with the library's promises. Additionally, they do not tolerate unprofessionalism and working alongside incompetent volunteers. They can always find another library or organization where their skills and talents will be valued.

Many of these young professionals tend to be tech-savvy. Their skills can be applied to help a library in unique ways. This new breed of volunteers does not want just to contribute. They want to apply their skills in ways that make them feel they are making a difference, especially since they give both their time and expertise.

As the definition of volunteers has evolved, so have the principles of volunteer management. Volunteer management can take time and effort, but the hard work and time are worth the results derived from this new breed of volunteers when the volunteer program becomes a success.

Principles of Volunteer Management

While it is easy to see volunteer management as getting a list of projects together and telling a volunteer "go and do this," it is often not that simple. Volunteer management is similar to managing a business or leading a group of people. People require guidance and leadership, and so do volunteers. The knowledge workers of today want to be led, motivated, and empowered. Influential leaders nurture and guide because they know how to empower people to use their gifts, talents, passion, and ideas to accomplish the mission. Effectively managing volunteers is the key to harnessing their enthusiasm for the benefit of the library. Presented below are some principles of volunteer management.

1. First, tap into the volunteer's motivational drives. When recruiting, interviewing, and training a new volunteer, take a moment to discover the person's motivation for volunteering in the library. Once a volunteer's motivation is clear, a volunteer manager or leader can build upon that motivation by providing the best type of reinforcement, encouragement, and recognition.

2. Second, be available. No one wants to work or volunteer without any communication or feedback. An influential leader is available to the persons they supervise. Being available is as simple as being in the library when the volunteer is there or responding to emails or texts from a virtual volunteer promptly. By being available, a volunteer manager can provide feedback, build rapport, encourage volunteers, and get projects organized, so the directions are clear or prepared to accommodate a volunteer.

3. Finally, never underestimate the power of food, fun, and laughter. Like paid staff, volunteers want to enjoy their work and have fun while accomplishing their tasks and duties. Hosting a short gathering of the volunteers and library staff to recognize a volunteer's contribution provides an opportunity to give public affirmation. Knowing the volunteers, their motivation for volunteering, and being available will allow each library to customize their volunteer management.

Rights and Duties of Volunteers

Understanding the rights, responsibilities, and duties of a volunteer is critical for a successful volunteer program. Planning while being aware of a volunteer's rights, responsibilities, and duties prepares the library as an institution to receive volunteers. This planning aligns the volunteer activities (work) into the overall library plans and organizational structure.

A library volunteer has the right to expect that his or her library duties represent meaningful work (not "make-do work") to the library's function. They need to know that their work contributes to the library's mission and strategic plan, that it can be completed in a reasonable time, and that it is ongoing, with tasks and duties defined by job descriptions and supported by staff expectations. These expectations are easy to achieve, provide a foundation for the volunteer to succeed, and allow the library to benefit from his or her work.

In addition to the fundamental rights listed above, a volunteer has the right to a designated workspace, input and some control about their assigned tasks, personal respect, orientation to the library, training, access to grievance procedures and conflict resolution, and recognition. If the volunteer is physically working in the library, he or she needs a designated workspace. The workspace can be small; however, consistency and accessibility to a designated workspace are vital. Nothing is more uncomfortable than starting a job and not having a designated workspace. Having to scramble and find a workspace is uncomfortable for the volunteer, and it communicates that the library did not plan ahead of time. A volunteer has the right to some control and input over the tasks assigned to him or her. When the volunteer participates cooperatively in determining his or her tasks, the volunteer can take ownership and be more committed to the library and its mission. Identifying the unique skills and gifts of volunteers can benefit the library and the volunteers. Any human being has the right to be respected as a unique individual; this holds true for an individual who has decided to volunteer and support the library.

As with new library staff members, a volunteer has the right to a minimum library orientation and training, including safety procedures. While the volunteer orientation and training scale may not be at the same level of detail and length as a library employee, these steps are essential for laying a strong foundation for the volunteer. By being in the physical space, the volunteer has the responsibility to follow established rules and policies. Lack of proper orientation and training leaves a volunteer figuring out the rules and policies independently, leading to the next right —access to grievance procedures and conflict resolution. When people work together, miscommunication and conflict occur. Volunteers have the right to access the library's established grievance procedures and conflict resolution processes.

Finally, a volunteer has the right to expect some recognition for his or her contribution. Recognition can be a simple spoken thank you, a handwritten note, an email, a text to the families of volunteers, or a formal luncheon or reception. The volunteer manager is responsible for knowing his or her volunteers and recognizing the best way to provide recognition.

A volunteer has responsibilities or duties to the library as well. Typically, a volunteer's responsibilities or duties are outlined in the position description, explained during the interview process, and listed on a volunteer agreement filed with a volunteer application. Examples of a volunteer's duties include:

- Performing duties as assigned to the best of one's abilities.
- Accepting guidance by the assigned staff member.
- Adhering to the appropriate library rules, policies, and procedures by wearing a name tag, dressing appropriately, maintaining customer confidentiality, and acting courteously to customers and staff.
- Reporting at the scheduled time.
- Giving prior notice to the volunteer manager if expecting to be absent or on extended leave.
- Giving notice upon terminating.
- Identifying any medical, health, or physical limitation related to the volunteer job.

Being familiar with the rights and duties helps prepare the library staff and volunteers for a meaningful experience.

Legal and Risk Management Issues

The legal and risk management concerns for library volunteers parallel similar concerns for paid library staff. At first, the legal and risk concerns can seem overwhelming, but breaking them down into specific areas of concern makes them achievable. The library's definition of volunteers will determine the areas of concern. For example, if the library decides that youth cannot be volunteers, youth volunteers' legal and risk management concerns will not apply.

For all types of volunteers, the volunteer recruiting process needs to be reviewed for any discrimination issues. Some libraries must follow the strict guidelines required for posting a paid library position, while other libraries can recruit more informally. All recruiting materials need to be professional and represent the library well. Libraries want to make sure that their volunteer recruiting process does not result in discrimination against certain types of volunteers (e.g., the disabled, specific racial minorities) that could result in a sensitive public relations problem. Each library must be aware and sensitive to local customs, laws, and cultural expectations.

If the library is willing to recruit volunteers with disabilities, library staff will need to be prepared to adapt tasks for a disabled volunteer. The umbrella of volunteers with disabilities may include adolescents and young adults who are developmentally disabled or brain-injured. In these cases, the library staff needs to have clear expectations and guidelines about the disabled volunteer's goal of volunteering. The goals of services or agencies representing disabled individuals might be quite different from the library's expectations. Planning is key in determining the library's definition of volunteers and having answers to various questions before disabled potential volunteers start showing interest.

A successful volunteer program can include recruitment of youth; however, the library staff will want to be familiar with all local employment regulations governing youth employment and the hours they may work. Many times, youth are interested in volunteering to complete their education and graduation requirements or meet a service group requirement. Another group of youth volunteers might be "youth at risk," which encompasses youth in trouble with law enforcement, youth with severe school problems, or both. These youth-at-risk volunteers will require more direct supervision, so the library staff must think through utilizing these volunteers and plan accordingly.

A final group of volunteers requiring additional planning is court-ordered workers. A local court system can use community service as part of the restitution process for individuals convicted of relatively minor offenses. This group of volunteers can be adult or youth. The formal paperwork and supervision for these volunteers will be more time-intensive.

Certain volunteer tasks determine specific types of legal and risk management issues a volunteer will need. These specific tasks include police reports, background and reference checks, driving records, and proof of insurance. If the volunteer represents the library off the premises (such as delivering books to individuals in their home), it is prudent to require a police report or background check. The library should require reference checks for volunteers, and this requirement needs to be in place for all types of volunteers. If a volunteer will be driving a library vehicle, the library needs to require a volunteer's driving record and proof of insurance.

Some final legal and risk management issues to consider before starting a volunteer program include hiring, health and safety regulations, general safety training, workers' compensation, customer confidentiality, termination interviews, de-volunteering, and a good Samaritan act. If volunteers work in the library space, the library staff must consider legal and risk management issues related to health, safety, and worker's compensation. For example, if a volunteer is watering a plant and spills water on the floor, the library is left open to a safety incident. Alternatively, if the volunteer slips and falls on the water and is injured, questions will arise. Does the volunteer provide his or her insurance, or does the library cover the medical expenses? Some countries have a good Samaritan act granting immunity from personal liability to volunteers in nonprofit and government organizations acting within the scope of their duties. Checking local laws and acts is advised. Termination interviews and de-volunteering questions are necessary as people can change their minds about volunteering. When a volunteer leaves, conducting a termination interview can provide helpful information to the library about improving the volunteer program. If the library needs to dismiss a volunteer, having de-volunteering processes and policies in place ahead of time will help in a sensitive situation.

While the legal and risk management issues can appear overwhelming, most libraries have similar policies and processes for their paid employees. Adapting existing policies and defining what type of volunteers the library seeks makes tackling the legal and risk management issues achievable.

Tips for Recruiting Volunteers

- Ask volunteers personally rather than relying on announcements. Recruiting volunteers is similar to asking someone to go on a first date. Remember that the library is not just looking for someone "to volunteer." Instead, the library is looking for someone to commit as a volunteer for the library.
- Similar to a first date, recruiting volunteers is a series of small steps leading to a commitment. Talk with the potential volunteers. Notice how they work, observe them, gather information, ask questions, and study their strengths and weaknesses. Be prepared before asking them to become a volunteer. On the first date, provide the volunteer with a taste of what committing to the library will be like and gather information about how they work. If the volunteer coordinator likes their help, he or she can ask them on a second date—people like being asked for their help.
- Develop strategic recruiting partnerships—build a network of a recruiting team. Do not go it alone.
- Recruit short-term project teams. The more specific the time limit, the more people are likely to help with a project. Moreover, short-term commitments might open the door to longer commitments.
- Assume that a "no" means "not now" or "not this position." Think of "no" as an opportunity to listen carefully to the reasons behind the "no."
- Develop roles and responsibilities or a position description for each position. Do not fill any position without finding the person who matches what the library needs.

- Recruit specific people for specific roles. Ask professionals to be in charge of significant areas of the library that represent what they love doing.
- If necessary and possible, hire dedicated volunteer managers – people who know and love volunteers and are ready to devote a good portion of their time to managing volunteers. Make sure they have a "positive volunteer attitude" (McKee 2012, 61).

Works Cited

Corporation for Community and National Service. 2006. *Volunteer Growth in America: A Review of Trends Since 1974.* Washington, DC. *https://generosityresearch.nd.edu/assets/13044/volunteer_growth.pdf.*

Driggers, P., and E. Dumas. 2002. *Managing Library Volunteers: A Practical Toolkit.* Chicago: American Library Association.

Lyttle, M., and S. Walsh. 2016. "The Challenge of Using Volunteers in the Library." In *Public Libraries Online. https://publiclibrariesonline.org/2016/11/the-challenges-of-using-volunteers-in-the-library.*

McKee, J., and T. McKee. 2012. *The New Breed: Understanding and Equipping the 21st Century Volunteer,* 2nd Edition. Group.

Nicol, E., and C. Johnson. 2008. "Volunteers in Libraries: Program Structure, Evaluation, and Theoretical Analysis." *Reference and User Services Quarterly* 48, no. 2: 154–63.

CHAPTER 6

Theological Library in the New Normal Environment: New Dynamics of Institutional Relationship

REYSA C. ALENZUELA AND MA. CYNTHIA PELEÑA

THE GLOBAL PANDEMIC HAS CHANGED THE COURSE OF HOW LIBRARIES FUNCtion, transforming the service delivery, collection, space, and facilities of theological libraries. While there are discussions on faculty-librarians' relationship, the value of the library committee and the need for cohesive library relationships with academic departments and other support offices are not fully engaged. This is much less in the conversations of theological librarians.

Hence, this empirical perspective from Henry Luce III Library (HLL) of the Central Philippine University hopes to provide insights on the role of faculty as members of the library committee and other stakeholders inside and outside the university.

To give a clearer view, we begin with the background of the institution. Central Philippine University is one of the leading universities in the central part of the Philippine archipelago and was founded in 1905. The university started as a mission institution in the 1900s (Central Philippine University, 2019) and has been strongly supported by the American Baptist Church. Hence, theological education has always been an important part of the institution. It is hoped that this empirical case of the University will illuminate a new paradigm of collaboration between librarians and faculty.

The library is under the Office of the Vice President for Academic Affairs as part of academic support. The library director supervises the total operation of the library and takes overall responsibility for the administration of library resources and services. There is a library committee composed of representatives from different academic departments who review policies and procedures in the library. The committee also plays an active role in collection development and promotion of library resources and services.

The minimum requirement for librarians is a bachelor's degree and professional licensure from the Philippines to practice librarianship. In academic libraries, they hold faculty status. Under the Philippine Association of Academic and Research Libraries's standards, a ratio of one librarian per department is practiced. Liaison librarianship has been strengthened recently, during the pandemic, as students and most of the faculty cannot go to the library.

As to collection development, the main goal is to support the mission, vision, goals, and objectives of the university, college, department, and programs. The members of the library committee are very important in this process as they liaise with the department on what new resources must be added. However, with the new normal, patterns of communication have changed. Faculty members directly request materials through chat and other online platforms.

With the shift to the online mode, the library services have also transformed, introducing virtual reference services (VRS) and providing online document delivery services. Social media platforms are also used to engage with users. Moreover, in terms of space and facilities, the library occupies a separate building. At present, the space is also used by faculty who conduct synchronous classes.

Linkages and collaboration in the library have existed for more than two decades. HLL is a member of Iloilo interlibrary loan consortium. This local library cooperation facilitates resource sharing and access to member libraries in the city. For international linkages, HLL is part of the World Bank Knowledge for Development Center in the region. HLL is also part of the dynamic network of American Corners—a resource center for reliable information about the United States. The network, which has an established section in the library called American Corner, allows the usage of databases that the American Spaces made available.

Discussion

The library aligns its services and functions with the university's mission, vision, goals, and core values. How it deals with internal relations, particularly with the theology department, is always guided by the core values of the university. With the onslaught of the pandemic, academic institutions need to address the demand of the changing times to be resilient and sustainable. Likewise, demands for changes dictate theological library services in the new work environment. In an essay on "Ecologies of Space in the Paradoxes of Technology and Community: Adaptability and Resilience in Libraries, Churches, and Theological Schools in a COVID-19 World," the author posed some of the relevant questions: "What, then, are the ways forward for churches, theological schools, and libraries in the current environment? What does it mean to have services of reference, circulation, and research in a theological library, but done completely through technological means, where patrons cannot do their work in the physical library?" (Elia 2020, 25–6). Libraries cannot stop performing their functions. Only the channels of communication might change. There is a need for a stronger, more cohesive relationship with faculty and the department in order for library services to be relevant. It is more than just a matter of technological concern—it is an issue of relationship, and this is where faculty-library connection must be strengthened.

Beyond compliance to standards, the value of the library committee has always been realized at Central Philippine University Henry Luce III Library. The "Charter of Library Committee" is a binding document that signifies the importance of faculty relations. In terms of organizational structure, the library committee is, in the same way as the entire library system, under the supervision of the vice president for academic affairs and is tasked to act in an advisory capacity to the university president and the director of libraries in library matters. A faculty representative from each college or department is appointed and the Theology Department has one representative.

The committee is responsible for informing the library about new education policies, new courses, and new members of the faculty, as well as staffing plans of the college. Moreover, the representative serves as an adviser and advocate to bridge the gap in communication between students and other faculty members. As the Charter of Library Committee describes, the committee is a "sounding board" of complaints. Having someone from the outside (of the library) to give their perspective on the position of the library builds more credibility in how the library endeavors to address the needs of the academic community.

Through effective and direct communication to the librarians, the library committee shares the sentiments of the library users to improve the services of the library. This committee also recommends development for the physical aspects of the library and the allocation of acquisition funds for the college. The members help determine priorities in acquisition and review and amend library policies to provide flexible, fair and equitable services underpinning inclusivity. The faculty representative's role in assisting in the review of policies on acquisition, including administration and control of special materials, is indispensable. Acquisition of resources, the majority of which have shifted from print to online, can be supported by the faculty liaisons.

The library committee also has a binding opinion on library participation in regional cooperative proposals or engagement in consortia. Decisions on acceptance of gifts and donations may also be referred to the committee. As to instruction, a key role of the library committee is to shape plans and programs to implement development of resources for instruction and research.

Studies have been done about faculty-librarian collaboration and the important role of the library committee. One of the local studies conducted a decade ago was the master's thesis of Cantel (2010) on the awareness and extent of participation of library committee members in the performance of their roles and functions. Roles highlighted included the assessment of collection strength, marketing, promotion, and coordination of the college/department needs. Faculty are aware of these roles but they often have other duties that prevent them from full participation in all of their potential functions. Moreover, aside from the library committee functions, other faculty-librarian dynamics were suggested by the researcher to be explored that can further realize the value of the library.

The current situation calls for reflection on new roles to be explored. As librarians reskill to become instructors teaching how students will find reliable resources, the pedagogical insights of faculty who are well-versed on the needs of the students can be very helpful. In some libraries, training on reskilling librarians to be instructional librarians is conducted by faculty as concepts of instructional design and learning assessment are not the forte of most librarians, particularly those who have little experience beyond their library and information science degrees. In the Philippines, such vertical alignment is highly regarded, but there can be some pitfalls when there are modifications in functions and integration of new roles.

Faculty Relations: Juxtaposing and Transcending

In the Philippines, discussion of faculty collaboration is mainly associated with compliance to standards. As mentioned above, one key area of program accreditation requires the creation of a library committee with representatives from each college or department. Hence, collaboration with the faculty and other stakeholders in theology departments is essential. Although the inception of the faculty committee came out of compliance to accreditation, the relationship that has evolved between the library and the stakeholders of the Theology Department is part of the organizational dynamics—brought about by the necessity to grow and with the same goal of providing for the needs of faculty and students. Faculty collaboration went beyond the faculty being representatives for their respective departments. Recently, a partnership between HLL and the Association of Theological Education in Southeast Asia (ATESEA) created the interaction of a networked paradigm where the library director, faculty, and ATESEA are mutually involved.

New Dynamics of Collaboration

Faculty and librarian relationships, in general, have a wide range of literature; however, faculty-librarian collaboration in theological libraries is very minimal and not as recent.

One interesting discussion about faculty-librarian relationship is McMahon's (2004, 75) essay on how faculty/librarian partnerships have changed at the University of Manitoba, where five areas for improved collaboration are identified: 1) teaching/instruction, 2) information services, 3) information technology, 4) research, and 5) collections.

New directions on teaching and learning call for reinvented faculty-librarian relationships. One significant initiative that has evolved in the promotion of theological education is a creative collaboration that goes beyond engagement with theology faculty and theological librarians/staff. Recently, HLL worked with Graduate School faculty in the Master in Library and Information Science-Theological Librarianship (MLIS-TL) program to expand its services—i.e., enhancing research and ensuring that the competence of theological librarians in Southeast Asia is responsive to the needs of theology departments. Having ATESEA spearhead and sponsor the program, avenues for discussion are amplified on how to address the challenges in online learning support.

While there is a faculty representative on the library committee, in most cases, the faculty go to the library director to request books to be purchased and to make sure that their information needs will be addressed. However, the need to have a point of contact at the department is essential as theology is a discipline that has distinct resources and research needs. An additional channel for coordination has not affected the role of the library committee representative but rather amplified what can be offered by the library.

On instructions, Paul Schrodt, in his speech at Atla's fiftieth anniversary, highlighted the function of the theological librarian as an educator and declared that the library is a "parallel educational arena" with the classroom (McMahon 2004, 74). As early as 1996, the role of theological librarians in educational support had been dubbed as "empowerers." Indeed, it is happening nowadays! With the transformation to online learning, the role of theological librarians as curators and educators is very much a necessity. Librarians are now at the forefront of research and instructions with their skills to retrieve and organize tools and resources. In a world where emerging technology is a primary commodity, a librarian's role goes beyond handling directional queries—which is giving exactly the resources sought for or pointing out where the resources can be found. The information environment becomes highly scalable and librarians need to teach the concept of searching and evaluating resources so that, with changes brought by new technology or an upgrade in the platform, the library users have the base knowledge to work independently.

Rhetoric of the New Normal

One of the fundamental questions to be addressed is how internal relationships are changing. With the new normal environment, will the old rules and governing standards still apply?

In the perspective of HLL, faculty-librarian relationships only changed from face-to-face to virtual communication. Similarly, as resources are converted to digital to avoid physical contact, more resources are delivered online. In fact, with the need to incorporate online resources, faculty need to engage more with librarians not only in request for resources but also in consultation about issues on copyright in the digital platform. Librarians can go beyond resource-sharing. Librarians in most academic institutions need to be curators and educators. Online resources need to be organized to cater to the needs of the faculty, which is providing services before they ask for it.

As to application of standards, the organizational structure has not changed. Only resources and service delivery need to be revisited.

Conclusion

The value of the library committee and the cohesiveness of the library's relationship with academic departments and other support offices is essential in order for the library to fully function. In order for the library to be responsive to the needs of the faculty, committee representatives must serve as a credible voice to share about the role of the library and to lead engagement with faculty. Likewise, it is an important assessment mechanism wherein faculty representatives can relate the needs of the department.

Works Cited

Cantel, Ana Mae. 2010. "Awareness and Extent of Participation of Library Committee Members in the Performance of Their Roles and Functions. Master's thesis, Central Philippine University.

Elia, Anthony J. 2020. "Ecologies of Space in the Paradoxes of Technology and Community: Adaptability and Resilience in Libraries, Churches, and Theological Schools in a COVID-19 World." *Atla Summary of Proceedings* 74: 19–31.

Mays, Antje. 2013. "Biz of Acq: Using Technology to Increase Collaboration Between the Library, Teaching Faculty, and the Campus At Large." *Against the Grain* 15, no. 5: 22.

McMahon, Melody Layton. 2004. "Librarians and Teaching Faculty in Collaboration: New Incentives, New Opportunities." *Theological Education* 40, no. 1: 73–87.

CHAPTER 7

Planning and Reporting

SIONG NG

STRATEGIC PLANNING IS OFTEN VIEWED AS TOO DIFFICULT OF A PROCESS TO execute and placed in the "too-hard" basket. It is especially challenging for small- to medium-sized libraries to devote sufficient staff time to plan, communicate, implement, and assess a strategic plan. The perception that strategic planning can only be designed by senior management is entirely inaccurate. Now, more than ever, theological libraries need to demonstrate their role and value to their parent institution. The main goal is to create a sustainable and achievable strategic plan that aligns with the institution's primary strategy. This chapter aims to present an easy guide for beginners to start the planning process, and to prepare, implement, and assess strategic plan progress during the year. Based on a gardener's metaphor, this chapter aims to encourage solo librarians and those who work in relatively small libraries in the developed or the majority world to set up and implement a strategic plan.

Why Is It Important?

The main aim of the process is to assure quality and assist in the continuous improvement of the library/organisation. A robust strategic plan in an academic setting adds value during the institutional accreditation process. Secondly, the strategic plan will assist with collection development planning that must be often evaluated due to the ever-changing landscape of the information environment. For non-academic libraries, the strategic plan can act as a direct plan to achieve desired goals by creating a more structural approach to managing tasks within a timeframe.

Strategic plans often begin after mission and vision statements have been created. What is the difference between mission and vision statements and the strategic plan? Haines et al. (2016, 132) state that a strategic plan focuses on a bigger scale. Roberts and Wood (2012, 10) define it as a "systematic process of envisioning a desired future and translating this vision into broadly defined goals or objectives and a sequence of steps to achieve them."

Alignment

Saunders (2016, 4) and Cottrell (2011) state that it is essential that the library's strategic goals align with the parent institution. To do this, it is crucial to identify the key themes in the institution's overall plans or goals. The library is part of the larger institution, depending on its support, including financially. Therefore, it is obligated to support and align its direction to the institution's mission and goals (Thompson et al. 2019, 49). The consequences of not aligning may result in disagreement, loss of direction, and financial impacts.

However, it is essential to note that it may be impossible to use all of the institution's goals and align them to the library's strategic objectives (Saunders 2016, 3). This is because not all of them are relevant or relate to the overall operation of the library.

In the absence of an institutional strategic plan, it is still recommended that conversation occurs between the library and the parent institution. This will potentially lead to a better outcome through adding the awareness of the library plan and allow the library to build congruently with the vision of the parent institution.

> **Helpful Tip** Be realistic about what you are trying to achieve. If your users will not view electronic resources because of the context where they are located, e-books are not necessary to address in your strategic plan.

In a non-academic environment, the organisation you are part of or associated with is the parent institution. For example, in a place of worship, one of the main goals of a congregational library might be to reach out to unemployed people in the community. Therefore, the role of the library could potentially be assisting this group of people in finding employment by providing books on writing a curriculum vitae and cover letters.

The authors of *Strategic Planning for Academic Libraries* suggest two main questions that can help the beginning stage of writing a strategic plan (Thompson et al. 2019, 48).

- What do we hope to achieve with our strategic plan?
- How will we know whether we have achieved it?

On top of the two questions above, I found the following question useful during the preparation:

- What are the core outcomes I would like to see?

There are several strategic planning models available. For example, Stephens (2017, 133-4) uses an integrated library planning model, which is based on an integrated business planning model. Stephens argues that it is less clingy, shorter, and appears to be more systematic. The remaining essay explores one way of setting up a strategic plan.

Step 1

For a gardener, the ground preparation work is essential. To have a substantial result, thorough research is needed, such as finding out about the soil—the conditions needed to flourish and thrive. The groundwork is to conduct an environmental scan. This can be done informally or formally, such as using the appreciative inquiry method (Stephens 2017, 134) through the following areas:

1. **Identify the core outcomes** the library desires to achieve. Be realistic on what you can achieve based on the organisation's capability and resources.

   Helpful Tip Limited budget on e-resources? One outcome could be setting up demand-driven acquisitions with several vendors (Goedeken and Lawson 2015).

2. **Read about the Association of College & Research Libraries (ACRL) top trends** to learn about current trends and where the library is heading in the coming years (ACRL Research Planning and Review Committee 2020). From the list, you may be able to select one or two trends that are relevant and align with your library and institution's desired outcomes.

   Helpful Tip Open access is listed as one of the trends. One outcome could be to identify the relevant titles and make them accessible to your users.

3. **Scan what is already out there and what is crucially needed.**

   Helpful Tip If one of your goals is to set up a toy library and there is already one well established in the neighborhood, is another one necessary?

Helpful Tip With coronavirus affecting most countries and how libraries provide their services to their users, one library outcome could be how your library can continue to provide services to your users in a safe environment.

There is no standard timeframe for how many years a strategic plan should cover. For small institutions, a suggested timeframe is two to three years. Haines et al. (2016, 138) indicate that the strategic plan is not a static policy or document. The plan can be edited, especially to remove items if they are longer relevant.

Step 2

A gardener will often research to identify the plants that are suitable for planting for the next season. The preparation work will occur before the season and before planting any seeds. One method of preparation in a strategic plan is to conduct a SWOT (strengths, weaknesses, opportunities, and threats) analysis in order to understand the library's current situation. This process does not require much planning. The facts are gathered from the formal or informal interviews from step 1 and from observing the situation around you. The beauty of this is that the points can be added or edited at any time. It can be done in a simple format, such as in a table or an Excel spreadsheet (Ebertz and Stutzman 2020, 126). Stutzman has set up an online strategic planning workbook that is easy to set up and follow.

Figure 1. Example of SWOT Analysis

Strengths	**Weaknesses**
Dedicated staff	The budget has been cut 10%
Opportunities	**Threats**
Outside funding is available	COVID Usage is going down

Step 3

After preparing the soil and knowing what to plant according to the season, the gardener is planting into the space allocated for it.

This stage of writing the strategic plan involves documenting the initiatives, action plan, and deadlines. From the outcomes, you will list one or more directions that can lead to the outcomes.

Figure 2. Example of a strategic plan (Sample Elements for

Focus	Outcomes	Initiatives
Student wellbeing	Ensure a safe environment for students	1.1 Review the library space and identify an area which it can be utilized for students to relax
		1.2 Staff attend relevant training in mental health or related topic

The next step is to identify the action and who is responsible for each task from the outcomes. The fun part of the strategic plan is that there are no standard templates or formats. Therefore, it is really up to each organisation to draw it up in a way that is easy to read and understand. Action plans and deadlines are in-house (shaded grey in the table below) notes and, therefore, not documented in the public strategic plan.

See figure 2, below:

a Strategic Plan, In-house Use, 2021–23)

Action Plan	Deadlines	Indicators
Library team to look at the layout and identify the spaces that can be used	All staff involved Deadline: December 2021	Consultations meeting with library staff. Satisfied outcome from the meeting Report with recommendations completed
Get input from the student body, such as members of the student association	Advertise and identify those students that can assist. AB and AC to advertise on Facebook and newsletters Deadline: July 2021 Set a time for the focus group and gather the feedback Deadline: September 2021	Number of students participated in the focus group Documented the feedback from the focus group
Source relevant workshops or courses	SH to research on relevant courses. Deadline: December 2021	Staff attended relevant training session conducted by the Mental Health association Organised Mental Health awareness week

Figure 2. Example of a strategic plan (Sample Elements for

Focus	Outcomes	Initiatives
Student wellbeing (cont'd)	Ensure a safe environment for students (cont'd)	1.3 Seek funding to purchase new furniture that provides a more welcoming space

Step 4

The gardener's next steps are to enhance productivity by watering, feeding, and trimming the plants regularly. The concept is similar in executing a strategic plan. Ongoing assessment is essential to be effective (Thompson et al. 2019, 53). Saunders (2016, 14) states that "if libraries are not assessing their strategic goals, then they are not establishing their value or holding themselves accountable to their communities." Moreover, it needs to be integrated into the strategic plan to affirm the value and accountability.

a Strategic Plan, In-house Use, 2021–23)

Action Plan	Deadlines	Indicators
Locate various furniture suppliers for ideas and quotes	AB to contact various suppliers. Deadline: March 2022	Number of quotes submitted Shortlist to two potential suppliers
Set up informal focus groups to get feedback from our users	AC to invite uses to be part of the focus group Deadline: June 2021	Number of stakeholders attended the focus groups Documented the feedback from the focus groups
Plan how the furniture will look in that space	AC will draw the plan with assistance from the supplier Deadline: October 2021	Plan submitted
AB to complete the funding application form	Deadline: August 2021 Two intakes a year	Funding application submitted

The year 2020 was a year of uncertainty—this a good example where regular review keeps the strategic plan relevant and current. The global pandemic affected the ways we deliver services to our library users. Information professionals were required to adjust what we are doing and to modify our core services and resources in a short time frame.

A change in leadership in the parent institution may affect the budget and the goals of the institution. Thompson et al. (2019, 49) state that it is essential to be ready for changes and events that will impact the planning process even after completing the strategic plan. Therefore, a strategic plan needs to have the flexibility to have room for adaptation when unpredictable events occur. At other times, the feedback you received from your stakeholders may result in a change of direction or the necessity to modify the outcomes or directions.

Conclusion

A more systematic approach will make the strategic planning process less daunting. It may seem a lengthy process, especially when there are other pressing day-to-day matters. However, the outcomes of a well-constructed strategic plan will be rewarding when you can see the results of the set goals. As Cicero put it, "if you have a garden and a library, you have everything you need."

Works Cited

ACRL Research Planning and Review Committee. 2020. "2020 Top Trends in Academic Libraries: A Review of the Trends and Issues Affecting Academic Libraries in Higher Education." *College & Research Libraries News. https://doi.org/10.5860/crln.81.6.270.*

Cottrell, Janet R. 2011. "What Are We Doing Here, Anyway? : Tying Academic Library Goals to Institutional Mission." *College & Research Libraries News* 72, no. 9: 516–20. *https://doi.org/10.5860/crln.72.9.8633.*

Ebertz, Susan, and Karl Stutzman. 2020. "Planning Strategically for Small Libraries." *Atla Summary of Proceedings* 74: 124–32. *https://doi.org/10.31046/proceedings.2020.1855.*

Goedeken, Edward A., and Karen Lawson. 2015. "The Past, Present, and Future of Demand-Driven Acquisitions in Academic Libraries." *College & Research Libraries* 76, no. 2: 205–21.

Haines, Darla, Rebecca Johnson, Jill Lichtsinn, and Edita Sicken. 2016. "Mission Possible: Strategic Planning for Small Academic Libraries." In *The Small and Rural Academic Library : Leveraging Resources and Overcoming Limitations,* edited by

Kaetrena Davis Kendrick and Deborah Tritt, 131–45. Chicago: Association of College and Research Libraries.

Roberts, Ken, and Daphne Wood. 2012. "Strategic Planning: A Valuable, Productive and Engaging Experience (Honest)." *Feliciter* 58, no. 5: 10–11.

Saunders, Laura. 2016. "Room for Improvement: Priorities in Academic Libraries' Strategic Plans." *Journal of Library Administration* 56, no. 1: 1–16. *https://doi.org/10.1080/01930826.2015.1105029.*

Stephens, Myka Kennedy. 2017. "Integrated Planning for Theological Libraries." *Atla Summary of Proceedings* 71: 133–40. *https://serials.atla.com/proceedings/issue/view/39/18.*

Thompson, Gregory C., Harish Maringanti, Rick Anderson, Catherine Soehner, and Alberta Comer. 2019. *Strategic Planning for Academic Libraries: A Step-by-Step Guide.* Chicago: ALA Editions.

CHAPTER 8

Forecasting Your Budget

CYNTHIA SNELL

EVERY NEW STUDENT ENTERING YOUR LIBRARY DOORS EACH YEAR EXPECTS your library to satisfy their needs. The needs of the students change and grow with every new class. In addition, the expectations of the community change and grow with every new program offering. However, the library budget does not always increase with the demand. Careful planning and evaluation before creating and implementing new services and resources will ensure that your funds are spent wisely.

So what does the term "budget" really mean? Investopedia defines a budget as "an estimation of revenue and expenses over a specified future period of time. . . usually compiled and re-evaluated on a periodic basis" (Ganti n.d.). The keyword here is "estimation." There is no way for us to determine the exact amount of need within the twelve months of each budget year. We can "estimate" what will be needed to supply the library community services and resources in the upcoming year. This is what I will refer to as "forecasting" future needs. How do we do this?

First, you need to understand the library mission, vision, and goals:

- Do you have clear mission, vision, and goal statements?

Second, you need to understand the budgeting process at your organization:

- Does your budget have elements that roll over, or do you start over each year?
- Is your next year's budget determined by the money you spent this year, or is it zero-based?
- Who approves your overall budget?

Third, you will want to understand what needs to be renewed:

- Are you paying for resources that are not being used?
- Are there new programs being offered?

Finally, you want to understand how you want to grow your services:

- Are there resource updates you would like to purchase?
- Are there improvements to the building that need to be made?

Understanding the Mission, Vision, and Goals

Understanding the library's mission and how that mission supports the organization's greater mission is extremely important when forecasting your next yearly budget. The mission tells the organization why the library exists; in essence, it is the library's identity and its association to the larger organization. The vision tells the organization what your library hopes to accomplish. Finally, the goals tell the organization how the library will continue its mission and achieve the vision. Therefore, having a vital mission, vision, and goals will help support any needs the library identifies for the following year. To understand how to create these statements, please refer to the chapter in this book written by Amy Limpitlaw entitled "Library Mission and Goals" (pp. 1 ff.).

Understanding the Budget Process

You might be saying, "why do I need to understand the overall budget process used by my organization?" Understanding your organization's overall budgetary process increases your ability to adequately develop a detailed forecast of what funds will be needed from year to year. For example, some organizations allow for specific unused budgetary allocations to roll over into the next year, while others start over each year. Your organization could do a combination of both within one budget. Understanding how your organization works will help you plan more efficiently. So, here we have two budget allocations:

Allocation Name	Current Year	Spent	Remainder
Bibles	2000	1500	500
Research Databases	13000	10000	3000

The allocation for "Bibles" rolls over each year, but the allocation for "Research Databases" does not. You spent $1500 of the $2000 you had budgeted for in this current year on Bibles. You are estimating you will be spending another $1500 next year. Since this is a roll-over account, that means your forecast would equal $1000 for next year because you still have $500 from this year which rolls over into next year. Since the research databases do not roll over, you will lose the $3000 remaining in your budget. Therefore, next year you know you will need to request a minimum of $10,000.

You also need to be aware of whether you need to create your forecast from what you spent this past year or whether your budget is zero-based, meaning what was spent last year has no bearing on what you request for next year. Using our Bibles and research databases example, a zero-based budget would not have to consider what was spent this year. You could request whatever amount you estimate your need to be for next year. However, if your budget is based on the funds used in the current year, you would likely request $1000 for Bibles (since you have $500 that rolls over) and $10,000 for research databases.

Finally, you will need to understand the approval process. Most often, the board of trustees will make the final decision as part of institutional planning for the following year. Let's look at an example:

Line Item Detail: Periodicals for LRC (10-1411-7025-ILLL)
To comply with CONTU regulations for ILL requests

This Request		**Jul 2020 – June 2021**
$2000 allocated up front		$2000 ($0.00) allocated manually
Jul	$2,000	$4727
Aug	$0	($273)
Sep	$0	($273)
Oct	$0	($273)
Nov	$0	($273)
Dec	$0	($273)
Jan	$0	($273)
Feb	$0	($273)
Mar	$0	($273)
Apr	$0	($273)
May	$0	($273)
Jun	$0	$0

Here is a real example of an expenditure that I assigned this past year. You can see that this expenditure is for the purchase of periodical subscriptions following the CONTU ("The Campus Guide to Copyright Compliance" n.d.) regulations surrounding interlibrary loan requests. This explanation's sole purpose is so that the Board of Trustees knows what the request refers to and why it is needed. The budgeting software your organization uses will determine how you will relay this information. The critical aspect is that you explain your requests.

In summary, the questions you need to answer before starting to create your forecast for the following year are:

- Does your budget have elements that roll over, or do you start over each year?
- Is your next year's budget determined by the money you spent this year, or is it zero-based?
- Who approves your overall budget?

After answering these questions, we now need to identify what is required to support your organizational community.

Understanding Need

Understanding need is probably the most difficult step in the budgeting process. This section will provide you with some indicators I have found to be useful when trying to identify needs: the collection age, new program offerings, interlibrary loan requests, and resource usage.

The age of your collection can be important for resources outside of theological and philosophical subject areas. These two areas never seem to lose their value due to age. They provide rich information that newer resources often do not. However, if you have subject areas like science or medicine, you will want to review outdated editions and calculate the price for more recent editions to replace the aging resources. You can use this estimate as part of the forecasted resource allocation for the following year.

You can also look at syllabi for updated resources used in courses and faculty purchase requests to determine resource allocations. For example, new program offerings also provide an opportunity to review your collection for resources that support the program. Resources can include research databases, journals, books, etc. Identifying a perceived need is probably the most difficult in forecasting cost. I currently find a wealth of information from reviewing syllabi for the course offerings within new and existing programs. The syllabi provide information about assignments that the student needs to complete, required and additional readings and often a bibliography of resources the students are encouraged to review. Using these areas can help move from a perceived need to informed forecasting.

Interlibrary loan requests also provide a wealth of information. These requests help to identify what topics are being researched and where your library collection has weak areas. For instance, we have 35 interlibrary loan (ILL) requests for resources focused on "educational social systems." When reviewing the LC191, which focuses on the social aspects of education, I found that we had only five items all of which were 30 years of age or older. The requests were all newer published items focused on student achievement, bullying, and peer pressure. We reviewed the cost of each if we were to purchase them and included 20 of the 35 titles in our forecasted budget. This list of titles and cost were then included in the details of the requested amount.

That brings us to usage evaluation. You will need to evaluate what you have purchased this past year, what resources are available to support each academic program, and what is actually being used by the community. Understanding what is being used gives you an idea of what your community needs. I have found I need to do this evaluation every year but on the past two years of data. Degree program class rotation goes on a two-year cycle; therefore, some resources may be required for the upcoming year even if they have been barely used during the current year. You will need to determine what is best for your library.

The best way to assess usage is by calculating the "return-on-investment" (ROI) for each subscription. Investopedia defines ROI as "tr[ying] to directly measure the amount of return on a particular investment, relative to the investment's cost" (Fernando n.d.). The resources you purchase are investments. Like any other investment, you want to be sure that you are investing wisely and your community is benefiting from those investments. To calculate the ROI, the cost is divided by the usage, which yields the amount you spend per usage. For example, I am evaluating the Atla databases to ensure that we want to continue subscribing to this research tool. The cost per year is $9300. Within the past year, there have been:

Sessions	Searches	Full-text requests	Abstract views
22336	57894	6737	4604

- Sessions = the number of times the database was launched
- Searches = the number of times search terms were entered
- Full-text requests = the number of times the full text of an article was downloaded
- Abstract views = the number of times an article's content was viewed online

So you may be asking, "which area is more important when doing your evaluation?" That is something you have to determine, but you want to use the same usage criteria for all your online subscription services. We look mainly at full-text and abstract views, which tells us the number of valuable articles available to our campus community in accordance to their needs.

9300 / 6737 = $2.11 per full-text article used this year.

Our acceptable cost also needed to be determined and used consistently across all online subscriptions. Ours is capped at $2 per use. Therefore, this database does not meet our ROI standards. However, when looking at the previous year, we spent $1.01 per full-text article. Therefore, we will retain this database for another year.

Let's review.

This is the budget estimation for databases that support the seminary. In this case, the Atla databases will be retained due to usage over two years that remains consistent with the established ROI.

Year	Database Sessions	Total Searches	Total Requests	Total Full-Text Requests	Abstract Requests
2020	22,336	57,894	11,513	6737	4604
ROI	$0.75	$0.28	$1.21	$2.11	$2.98

Year	Database Sessions	Total Searches	Total Requests	Total Full-Text Requests	Abstract Requests
2019	28,055	73,996	15,934	9250	6438
ROI	$0.33	$0.13	$0.58	$1.01	$1.44

Understanding Growth

Estimating the additional funds needed to accomplish your growth plan can be the most difficult to prepare. Whether it is additional subscriptions or structural repairs/additions, the cost is never definitive, and quotes can be time-sensitive. However, growth is a necessity if the library is to stay viable to the organization.

Additional resources that have been identified due to the age of the collection or new program offerings are important to include in your budget forecast. So, you will need to get quotes for these resources.

Structural repairs and additions are areas that are very important for you to include in your budget forecast. However, this forecast would actually be part of your capital funding. Capital funding is explained in more detail in the chapter authored by T. Patrick Milas entitled "Financial Accountability and Record-keeping" (pp. 81 ff.). For this section, I would just advise you to discuss these changes with your supervisor before including them in your forecast. Capital budgets often have other requirements that your operational budget does not.

Most importantly, *breathe*. Forecasting your budget is not an exact science. Experience does not mean you will never under- or over-forecast. Predicting the future always has unforeseen variables!

Works Cited

"The Campus Guide to Copyright Compliance." n.d. Accessed May 4, 2021. *https://www.copyright.com/Services/copyrightoncampus/content/ill_contu.html.*

Fernando, Jason. n.d. "Return on Investment (ROI) Definition." Investopedia. Accessed May 4, 2021. *https://www.investopedia.com/terms/r/returnoninvestment.asp.*

Ganti, Akhilesh. n.d. "Budget." Investopedia. Accessed May 4, 2021. *https://www.investopedia.com/terms/b/budget.asp.*

CHAPTER 9

Financial Accounting and Record-keeping

T. PATRICK MILAS

LIKE MANY ASPECTS OF ADMINISTRATION, FINANCIAL MANAGEMENT IS A matter of utmost discernment—but, when standardized, it facilitates earnest and transparent stewardship of our libraries' physical resources. Developing routine ways of executing and reporting business processes is the most sustainable method for an administrator to balance service to theological mission with service to financial wealth—"to serve God and money" (Matt. 6:24).

Robust financial management in theological libraries requires both macroeconomic and microeconomic analysis and documentation. At the broader, macroeconomic level for the library, the entire ecosystem of the library community environment is at hand, including historic and ideological precedents for preserving and investing in specific assets (e.g., prestigious geographic locations for facilities, proximity to denominational archives), systems (LC/Pettee/Dewey), and even workflows (in-house acquisitions and cataloging). Many of these idiosyncratic commitments force theological libraries today to "live beyond their means," using a gradual draw on their institutions' endowments to afford business-as-usual. Financial accounting in higher education is more relaxed than in the corporate world. While a hard-boiled financial auditor may provide gloomy outlooks for the institution as a whole, it is the theological library administrator's charge to responsibly steward what resources remain available at present. Note: all examples in this chapter originate from the Gardner A. Sage Library at New Brunswick Theological Seminary (NBTS) where the author is the library director (chief administrative officer).[1]

At the microeconomic level, financial accounting involves reference to two principal asset types: fiscal resources and human resources. For accounting purposes, fiscal resources are classified as either budget resources (e.g., reserves, investments) or operating resources (e.g., tuition income, interest on endowments). Operating resources or the operating budget is what theological library administrators manage day-to-day.

Some generally accepted accounting principles should undergird the financial accounting of the theological library's operating budget, including precedents for accurate representation, consistency, full disclosure, relevance, timeliness, and verifiability. Accurate representations are neutral and free from error. Consistent accounting is executed in a routine, predictable way. Full disclosure provides enough information for stakeholders to make prudent decisions. Relevant accounting includes all details that could impact decision-making. Timeliness ensures that accounting documentation is made available when the data is still actionable. When all of the library's records can be confirmed as accurately represented, they are considered verifiable.

These accounting principles are generally applied whenever you record transactions and events, or adjust capital assets (discussed later). The fiscal year at NBTS is July to June instead of January to December, as is common in business. The usefulness of credit varies with the academic lifecycle; in North American schools on two-semester schedules, there is a substantial lull in revenue from May until August when student tuition monies begin to be received for the fall semester. Regardless of when a financial event occurs, a standard order should be applied. The most common approach is the first-in, first-out cost flow assumption; provided that a due date has not passed and funds are available, the first expense incurred should be the first expense paid.

There are two main overlaps between fiscal resources and human resources—times when individuals carry special importance as either fiscal assets or as liabilities.

Macro-stakeholders such as board members, corporate donors, and alumni are certainly a form of social wealth that can translate to fiscal wealth upon donation and estate behests. Micro-stakeholders, including current students (FTEs) and faculty/staff, can be forms of fiscal wealth and liability. Tuition monies paid by students are assets. Scholarships given on students' behalf and faculty/staff salaries are clear liabilities. Library resource subscription costs vary according to the present quantity of matriculated users (FTEs), so students, faculty, and staff are all fiscal liabilities in the library's financial management.

Theological librarianship also necessitates thinking beyond the macro and micro to the financial costs and benefits to resource sharing through consortia. For comparatively large institutions (such as Princeton Theological Seminary) dedicated to exhaustive collection development in theological subjects (especially biblical studies), this means sharing resources in biblical studies will be more of a cost than a benefit. For small institutions (like NBTS, committed to robust collection in the Reformed tradition and preservation of the unique Dutch Reformed ephemera), resource sharing will be more of a benefit than a cost.

Financial accounting involves accountability. Accountability to the institution requires the library administrator execute library operations with fiduciary integrity; administrators are fully responsible for the accounting they report and the records they keep. Depending on location, they may be legally and professionally liable for their library's accounting practices. Transparency is also critical for accountability to library staff. Administrators should keep staff well-informed about the library budget's sub-accounts relevant to their positions. Budget reports should be made available on a regular basis throughout the year, and staff should be included in annual budget proposal planning. At the institutional level, accountability also refers to the ethical investment of fiscal resources. Given the Christian ethic that guides all NBTS activity, special attention is given to avoid any investments that support or benefit from the arms trade, alcohol manufacturing and distribution, and private prisons.

Communication is key to effective financial reporting. A robust apparatus such as Microsoft 365 allows for reliable and consistent financial documentation with Microsoft Excel, Word, and PowerPoint. With this suite of applications, one can record debits and credits, compare them with worksheets from the seminary accountant or business office, and generate charts and graphs to share with library staff, donors, accreditors, and the administration in charge of budget proposal review.

There is a symbiotic relationship between the institution's finances and the library's finances. Budget reports are often prepared by the institution's business office for all departments within the institution. For example, reports on Sage Library's finances come from the chief financial officer at NBTS. Reports may be readable in a variety of formats. Standard monthly reports will typically display seven columns: three columns for activity from the most recent month and four for the year overall, including variance and actual. By observing when continuing costs are incurred for monthly and annual expenses, the library budget manager (usually the library director) can anticipate when funds will need to be available in the future. The greater care the library budget manager takes with financial reporting throughout the year, the easier the annual budget proposal preparation process should be. Library budget proposals may be presented in stages to a dean, provost, or president, but will ultimately be closely considered by the institution's chief financial officer in its business office.

Frequency of budget reporting varies among institutions. At NBTS, the chief financial officer distributes financial statements to budget managers, including the library director, on a monthly basis, whereas trustees receive quarterly reports. A theological library administrator should review recorded transactions at least once monthly; you cannot react effectively to irregularities if you are not promptly aware of them. Within the first two weeks after an erroneous accounting entry is made is the ideal period for disputing and correcting contractual charges from library vendors. Administrators with professional and paraprofessional direct reports are encouraged to include library staff not only in budget report review for specialized accounts, but also in annual budget planning.

Many institutional budgets are organized into unrestricted and restricted funds. Besides tuition revenue and donations, there are two types of restricted funds from which library expenses may be paid directly. The first is interest income from the NBTS endowment. This income is generally restricted to expenses very directly associated with student benefit, such as scholarships. The second comes from reserves, including interest income from reserves money and reserves money itself. The source of the extant reserves was the sale of valuable NBTS real estate to its neighbor, Rutgers University. A percentage limit is set by the board of trustees for how much may be spent from reserves without further consultation and approval by the board. When endowment and reserves monies are not being deployed to necessary expenses, they are otherwise invested in a portfolio array that includes US Treasury bonds, stocks, and mutual funds.

Sage Library's finances are also directly tied to both the reserves fund and the endowment fund. Specifically, the McDonnell Fund for medieval literature. The McDonnell Fund originates from the estate of a patron benefactor. It operates as a temporary, restricted fund. It is restricted because spending from it is primarily limited to the interest on the principal sum, and the expenses must pertain to medieval studies as outlined in the bequest. It is temporary because the opportunity to spend the interest has a two-year window, after which any interest remaining at the end of the second fiscal year is transferred to the general endowment.

Some library assets are expected to appreciate while others depreciate. Anticipating resources' future value is necessary when deciding how to record transactions in the general ledger and whether to "capitalize" them. Capitalizing expenses allows the institution to recognize the expense over a longer period of time than the date when a cost incurred. Assets such as modern library construction are capitalized for forty years—the expected longevity of the construction before major repairs or renovations will be necessary. Historic library building construction may have monetary value beyond its immediate usefulness as a functioning library.

For example, the Sage Library last appraised for nineteen million dollars but, in various ways, was deemed priceless or incalculable by the appraisal firm. Insurance is maintained at five million—a figure NBTS could use to construct a functional but less beautiful and historically significant library. So, the building is an asset that is expected to appreciate due to its historic and aesthetic qualities. However, the $500,000 that was raised through donations to complete repairs and necessary maintenance and install an accessible ramp in 2016 is expected to depreciate. Large expenses such as the building renovation, a new boiler ($40,000), and even labor costs for recent shelving are capitalized. Building expenses can be depreciated over a forty-year period, since a building can be expected to survive forty years of use. By contrast, purchases of the latest technology, including computers, are set to depreciate every three years due to expected obsolescence. Institutions use a variety of accounting approaches for book inventories. When the book inventory was maintained as a capital asset, anticipated depreciation was estimated based on shelf life and copyright expirations. At NBTS, the book inventory was written off years ago, so its balance sheet is now zero.

At NBTS, purchases under $1000 are automatically considered expenses; they are debited from the operating budget and are not capitalized. Asset transactions may be capitalized for a one-year period by recording them as a pre-paid account. This approach is relevant for research database subscription annual fees that may be paid in full but divided by twelve so that they affect the operating budget ledger at an equivalent rate each month. The library director submits invoices and receipts to the business office manager who records these entries electronically using Blackbaud software. The chief financial officer then analyzes and approves them on an ongoing basis.

At all levels of financial management, responsible documentation or record-keeping is critical. Record-keeping is not the same as record retention; records must be kept accurately, but many financial records need not be permanently retained. The thoroughness of record-keeping varies according to libraries' budgets for personnel and automation. Digital record-keeping with cloud hosting is an excellent way to retain and preserve critical financial information. Some institutional workflows may necessitate a print-based culture, so there would be an added expense of paying someone to scan and organize documents that are born and processed in print.

Records retention schedules vary due not only to requirements of regional/national governments and accreditation agencies but also to a library's provision for physical/digital space. At my institution, physical records continue to be kept for two years in locked file cabinets in the business office. Seven years' worth are kept in archival storage (which happens to be housed in the library).

Financial management, accounting, and record-keeping are usually absent from library and information science and theological education. Yet these processes are central to the effectiveness of any theological library administrator. If you are interested in exploring these topics further, consider a basic course in accounting from a nearby college or online. By all means, use colleagues as resources, too. If you have library-specific financial questions, ask a director from your regional or national theological library association. If you are new to administration and seek to understand the record-keeping approach you inherited, you could ask your predecessor about how records were kept. For issues where library and institutional finances intersect, dialogue with your chief financial officer, bursar, business office, or even the external auditor/consultant most familiar with your context. When routinized, documented, and well-understood, financial accounting and record-keeping can be marvelous lenses through which to celebrate the intellectual wealth you administer.

Notes

1 NBTS Chief Financial Officer Kenneth Termott is an invaluable conversation partner in all financial matters in my management and reporting of the Sage Library's finances. Special thanks go to Kenneth for his support in clarifying terminology and workflows useful for this chapter.

Contributors

REYSA ALENZUELA, MLIS, PhD, teaches at Central Philippine University in the Master in Library and Information Science program (MLIS and MLIS in Theological Librarianship). She is currently the head of the Scientific Library of the Oriental Institute of the Academy of Science in the Czech Republic. Prior to joining this research institute, she was a senior librarian of the University of the South Pacific Emalus Campus, Republic of Vanuatu, an expert manager at Nazarbayev University in Kazakhstan, and the director of the Thomas Jefferson Information Center at the US Embassy in Manila. She has published books and journals in library and information science and recently worked in developing the competency index for theological librarians in Southeast Asia.

KELLY CAMPBELL is associate dean of information services/senior director of the John Bulow Campbell Library at Columbia Theological Seminary located in Decatur, GA. Campbell holds a Master of Library Science degree, a Master of Arts degree in theological studies, and a Doctor of Education degree in organizational leadership from Pepperdine University. She serves as a member of the Association of Theological Schools Accreditation Teams and is chair of the Atla

International Theological Librarian Education Taskforce. In the past, she served two terms on the board of Atla, including the position of president, chaired the Atla Education Committee, and was a member of the Atla executive director search team. Campbell's global involvement includes attending the 2015 International Federation of Library Associations (IFLA) in Cape Town, South Africa, co-hosting a satellite meeting for the Religions: Libraries and Dialogue Special Interest Group satellite meeting in Ohio, and presenting at the Forum for Asian Theological Librarians Conference, the Philippine Theological Librarian Association, and the Australian/New Zealand Theological Librarian Association (ANZTLA). When not traveling and teaching, she enjoys quilting, cooking, and reading.

JAEYEON LUCY CHUNG, PhD., MLIS, is director of the Styberg Library and assistant professor of pastoral theology at Garrett-Evangelical Theological Seminary in Evanston, Illinois. She received her PhD in practical theology from Emory University in 2008, and her MLIS from Dominican University in 2011. Prior to her current position, Chung worked as technical services librarian at Garrett. She served, or still serves, on several professional committees: Atla's Diversity, Equity, and Inclusion (DEI) Committee (member, 2013–15; chair 2015–16), Atla's Board of Directors (2016–18), Association of Chicago Theological Schools (ACTS) Library Council (chair 2019–21), and *Journal of Pastoral Theology* Editorial Board (2017–present). She participated in the Wabash Colloquy on the Role of Theological School Librarians (2013). She also published her first book, titled *Korean Women, Self Esteem, and Practical Theology: Transformative Care* (Palgrave Macmillan, 2017) as well as articles in the areas of pastoral care, pastoral theology, and theological librarianship.

ANDREW KECK is the executive director of strategic initiatives and special assistant to the dean of Perkins School of Theology at Southern Methodist University. He previously served as associate director of Duke Divinity School Library and director of Luther Seminary Library. A longtime member of Atla, he was one of the founding editors of the open access journal *Theological Librarianship* and served as president of the Board of Directors in 2012–13.

AMY LIMPITLAW is head librarian at the School of Theology Library at Boston University. Prior to coming to Boston University in 2011, she held librarian positions at the Yale University Divinity School Library and at the Divinity Library at Vanderbilt University. She began her career as a librarian at the Boston Athenaeum. Amy earned a BA in religion from Trinity College, an MA in divinity, a PhD in theology from the University Chicago, and an MLIS from Simmons University. A longtime member of Atla, she has served on the Board of Directors and has given numerous presentations on different aspects of theological librarianship.

T. PATRICK MILAS is the director of the Gardner A. Sage Library and assistant professor of theological bibliography and research at New Brunswick Theological Seminary. He earned an BA degree in religion from Davidson College and MS and PhD degrees in library and information studies from Florida State University. For the last twenty-two years, he has served in academic, public, and government libraries, most recently at Princeton Theological Seminary. He enjoys harnessing the latest bibliographic management and biblical research technology for his research and integrating them to teach research methods. Recent courses taught include: Jewish Texts and Traditions; Contemplation and Social Justice; Social Science Research Methods; and Spirituality of the Twelve Steps. His research focuses on intersections of religion, technology, and libraries. Milas serves on the vestry at Trinity Episcopal Church in Cranford, New Jersey.

SIONG NG is the library manager at Carey Baptist College in Auckland, New Zealand. She was the president of the Australia and New Zealand Theological Library Association (ANZTLA) from 2015–18. She has presented papers at various conferences, including twice at Atla Annual, and has written a number of journal articles. Siong holds a bachelor's degree in music and a master's degree in information and library studies and music.

MA. CYNTHIA T. PELEÑA, MLIS, is currently the director of libraries at Central Philippine University. Before her appointment, she served as program coordinator of the Master in Library Science with specialization in Theological Librarianship (MLIS-TL), Master in Library and Library Science (MLIS), and Bachelor of Library Science (BLIS) degree programs from 2013–19 and as a part-time faculty member under the School of Graduate Studies, College of Education, and the College of Computer Studies at Central Philippine University. She graduated with a Master in Library and Information Science degree from Central Philippine University in 2010. In 2017, Cynthia received a professional enhancement grant as a visiting professor at Columbia Theological Seminary, Decatur, Georgia, USA, from July–September 2017. Currently, she is a member of the International Theological Librarianship Education Task Force (ITLE) under the American Theological Library Association from 2018 to the present.

KATHARINA PENNER was born in Soviet Kyrgyzstan and moved to Germany as a teenager. She holds two master's degrees—in theology as well as in library and information studies—and works toward a PhD in theological education. For the past thirty years, she has worked at theological schools in St. Petersburg, Russia, in Prague, Czech Republic, and in Austria, as a faculty member as well as library director. Since 2016, she has served as coordinator for library development at the Eurasian Accrediting Association and been involved in several writing projects as an author as well as coordinator.

CYNTHIA SNELL's education includes degrees from Penn College and Bucknell University as well as an MS degree in instructional/information technology from Bloomsburg University; an MS in library science from Clarion University; an MA in pastoral counseling and an MBA (leadership cognate) from Liberty University. In 1999, her academic career began as a reference assistant at Bucknell University. Cynthia moved to California in 2004 to accept a position as systems administrator and web designer for California Lutheran University. Upon moving to South Carolina in 2011, she accepted a position at Columbia College as library systems administrator and cataloger, which later expanded to include roles as distance education course administrator, electronic resource manager, and collection development/acquisitions manager. Cynthia joined the Columbia International University Library team as cataloger in 2015, and soon became the head of technical services. In July of 2016, she took the position of library director. She also serves as online studies course designer.

www.ingramcontent.com/pod-product-compliance
Lightning Source LLC
LaVergne TN
LVHW051014080826
845145LV00009B/2619
* 9 7 8 1 9 4 9 8 0 0 2 4 1 *